Happy #66 Dad
I hope it's got lots of Kicks

Love,

ESSENTIAL MILITARIA

NICHOLAS HOBBES

ESSENTIAL
Militaria

Facts, Legends, and Curiosities
about Warfare through the Ages

Grove Press
NEW YORK

Originally published as *Essential Militaria* by Atlantic Books,
an imprint of Grove/Atlantic Inc, Ltd.

Published simultaneously in Canada
Printed in the United States of America

FIRST AMERICAN EDITION

Library of Congress Cataloging-in-Publication Data
Hobbes, Nicholas.
Essential Militaria : facts, legends, and curiosities about warfare
through the ages / Nicholas Hobbes.
p. cm.
ISBN 0-8021-1772-4
1. Military history—Miscellanea.   2. Military art and
science—Miscellanea.   I. Title.
D25.H56 2004
355—dc22   2003067795

Grove Press
841 Broadway
New York, NY 10003

04   05   06   07   08   10   9   8   7   6   5   4   3   2   1

I Dedicate
to the
VIRTUOUS

these Volumes
Spirit of
LIBERTY.

Poor Reasons for War

1. FRENCH PASTRIES: In 1838, a squadron of French warships was sent to extract compensation from the fledgling nation of Mexico for French business losses during recent rebellions. One claim was for pastries taken from a restaurant by Mexican leader Santa Anna's troops. The resulting conflict was known as the War of the Cakes.

2. A DETACHED EAR: The War of Jenkins' Ear was named after Robert Jenkins, a British sea captain, who claimed that Spanish coast guards had cut off his ear in 1731. His exhibition of the ear in the House of Commons inflamed public opinion against the Spanish and war was declared in 1739.

3. LOSING A SOCCER MATCH: In 1969 a border dispute turned into a war when El Salvador's football team scored a last-minute winner against neighboring Honduras in a 1969 World Cup play-off. Hostilities began within hours and the Soccer War was to leave 3,000 dead and 6,000 wounded.

4. SELLING NEWSPAPERS: Press magnate William Randolph Hearst gave his *New York Journal* the edge in a circulation war with the rival *World* by launching a successful campaign for U.S. intervention in the Cuban struggle for independence, leading to the Spanish-American War of 1898.

5. POSTAGE STAMPS: When Bolivia issued a postage stamp featuring a map of its territory that included the disputed border region of Gran Chaco, Paraguay responded by issuing a larger stamp, including Chaco in its own map. The stamps

became bigger and bigger until the two sides came to blows in 1932.

6. A GREEDY PIG: The Pig War of 1860 almost broke out on the U.S.-Canadian border, which a Canadian pig kept crossing in order to eat American potatoes. When an American farmer shot the beast, a British warship was dispatched to San Juan resulting in a standoff with sixty U.S. soldiers. Fortunately, the commanders of each side agreed to stand down.

7. BULL ENVY: According to the Irish legend of the War of the Brown Bull, Queen Medb of Connaught was jealous of her husband's great bull Finnbhennach ("white-horned"), so she led armies from four provinces to capture the bull Donn from an Ulster chieftain.

Delicacies of War

Eaten by the *Daily News* correspondent Henry Labouchère during the Siege of Paris by the Germans in 1870.

1. Roast cat (tasted "like squirrel . . . delicious")
2. Kittens in onion ragout ("excellent")
3. Donkey steaks ("like mutton")
4. Rat salami ("something between frog and rabbit")
5. Spaniel slices ("by no means bad, something like lamb")

The Seven Past Lives of General George S. Patton

In his past lives, General Patton believed he was:

1. A prehistoric mammoth hunter
2. A Greek hoplite who fought the Persians
3. A soldier of Alexander the Great at the siege of Tyre

4. Hannibal
5. A Roman legionary under Julius Caesar
6. An English knight during the Hundred Years' War
7. A Napoleonic marshal

Disciplinarians

1. SHAKA: The Zulu king so disliked slow marchers that he would spear the last man in every column on the way to a battle.
2. GENERAL GEORGE S. PATTON: Slapped and punched shell-shocked soldiers and threatened them with his pistol, telling one artilleryman, "Hell, you are just a goddamned coward, you yellow son of a bitch. Shut up that goddamned crying. I won't have these brave men here who have been shot seeing a yellow bastard sitting here crying. You're a disgrace to the army and you're going back to the front to fight, although that's too good for you. You ought to be lined up against a wall and shot. In fact, I ought to shoot you myself right now, goddamn you!"
3. DUKE OF WELLINGTON: Was against the abolition of flogging in the British army, believing it to be necessary and better than putting men in detention where they would be unavailable for duty.
4. LYCURGAS OF SPARTA (C. 800 B.C.): Founder of the Spartan "constitution" and, by extension, father of the practice of encouraging gay sex for soldiers as a means of bonding.
5. BRIGADIER GENERAL ANDREW ATKINSON HUMPHREYS: This leader of a Union army division at Gettysburg was a maestro of bad language. Charles Anderson Dana, the assistant secretary of war, thought him "one of the loudest swearers" he had ever known, a man of "distinguished and brilliant profanity."
6. XERXES OF PERSIA: According to Herodotus, when the tyrant's first attempt to build a pontoon bridge across the Hellespont in 480 B.C. was ruined by a storm, he had the waters whipped in punishment.

7. LEON TROTSKY: During the Russian civil war of 1918–20, Trotsky formed "blocking detachments" behind the front lines in order to shoot soldiers who attempted to retreat.

8. LAVRENTI BERIA: Under the stewardship of Beria, the Soviet Union's NKVD secret police sentenced 400,000 Russians to service in the penal battalions during World War II. These units were used for suicide missions, such as the clearing of minefields by walking through them en masse.

9. JOSEPH STALIN: After the purge of the officer cadre in 1937, three of the Red Army's original marshals and thirteen of fifteen army commanders were dead, and 55 percent of divisional and brigade commanders, 80 percent of all colonels, and 43 percent of all other officer ranks had been executed.

Gays in the Military

Commanders reputed to be actively homosexual or bisexual.

Achilles
Leonidas of Sparta
Alexander the Great
Julius Caesar
Richard the Lionheart
Saladin
William of Orange
Frederick the Great
Lawrence of Arabia

The Eccentricities of Thomas J. "Stonewall" Jackson

1. HYPOCHONDRIA: Concerned with his digestion, he brought his own food to parties—usually crusts of stale bread. Jackson once

told a hostess that a single grain of pepper caused him to lose strength in his left leg.

2. BODY-IMAGE DISORDER: Believing his left arm heavier to be than his right, Jackson often kept it raised so that the blood would flow out and make it lighter and so restore his body's balance. He also believed he had an abnormal arrangement of internal organs; he obsessed over his posture and never allowed his shoulder blades to touch the back of a chair, nor would he bend over for fear of compressing his innards. His stiff posture no doubt helped achieve a military bearing.

3. LEMON SUCKING: It was said that he sucked on lemons constantly during battle, and today his admirers toss lemons inside the fence surrounding his statue in Lexington, Virginia. The stories are exaggerated; he actually preferred peaches.

4. BATHING: He bathed in ice-cold water.

5. OBEDIENCE: During his first year at the Virginia Military Institute Jackson continued to wear his heavy winter uniform into the spring season, explaining that he had received no order to change and that he would not do so until instructed by the superintendent. Once ordered to await the superintendent in his office, Jackson remained through the night because his superior had forgotten about the meeting.

6. INFLEXIBILITY: While teaching at the Virginia Military Institute, his standard lesson plan was to memorize a section from a textbook and then recite it to his class. If anyone asked a question he would simply recite the passage again, and again.

7. PIETY: He would never drink, smoke, dance, curse, play cards, or attend the theater. Neither would he send a letter if it meant that it would travel on a Sunday. Jackson regarded fighting on a Sunday as one of the chief reasons for his only major defeat at Kernstown.

Other Civil War Eccentrics

CSA LIEUTENANT GENERAL RICHARD EWELL: Stonewall Jackson's successor fidgeted constantly and would blurt out random sentences and expletives in the middle of a conversation. He slept cuddling a tool and would eat only wheat boiled in milk to assuage an imaginary disease.

CSA LIEUTENANT GENERAL JUBAL EARLY: A possible early sufferer of Tourette's syndrome, prone to bouts of incessant swearing.

CSA MAJOR GENERAL ISAAC TRIMBLE: Dressed as a dandy in cord and feathers, but was said to possess the loudest shouting voice in the Confederate army.

CSA BRIGADIER GENERAL ALBERT PIKE: Obsessed with mysticism and esoteric texts.

U.S. MAJOR GENERAL JOSEPH HOOKER: Ran his headquarters as what one observer described as "something between bar-room and brothel."

U.S. MAJOR GENERAL WINFIELD SCOTT HANCOCK: Obsessed with appearance and would change soiled shirts even during a battle.

U.S. LIEUTENANT GENERAL ULYSSES S. GRANT: Hated the sight of blood so much that his meat had to be cooked very well done. He also drank heavily.

U.S. REAR ADMIRAL DAVID D. PORTER: Would board his ship by galloping from the shore on horseback and leaping onto the deck.

Nicknames for the U.S. Marines

1. SOLDIERS OF THE SEA: A phrase first used to describe the British seaborne troops of the seventeenth century.
2. LEATHERNECKS: Referring to the leather collars used in the nineteenth century for protecting the neck and keeping Marines' heads erect on parade.

3. GYRENES: A derogatory term bestowed by the U.S. Navy around 1900, formed from a combination of "GI" and "Marines."
4. DEVIL DOGS: Coined by the Germans who fought them in 1918.
5. JARHEADS: A derogatory term from World War II, referring to the image presented by the Marines' high-collared dress uniform.
6. THE PRESIDENT'S OWN: Extended from its original reference to the Washington, D.C. Marine band, which plays at official functions.
7. AMERICA'S 911 FORCE: Used because the Marines are the first troops to be called upon in times of crisis (911 being the American emergency telephone number).
8. FARESTA: Meaning "Sea Angels" and given to the Marines by Bangladeshi flood victims in 1991.

The U.S. Marine Corps Rifleman's Creed

"This is my rifle. There are many like it, but this one is mine. It is my life. I must master it as I must master my life. Without me, my rifle is useless. Without my rifle, I am useless. I must fire my rifle true. I must shoot straighter than the enemy who is trying to kill me. I must shoot him before he shoots me. I will. My rifle and I know that what counts in war is not the rounds we fire, the noise of our burst, or the smoke we make. We know that it is the hits that count. We will hit. My rifle is human, even as I am human, because it is my life. Thus, I will learn it as a brother. I will learn its weaknesses, its strengths, its parts, its accessories, its sights and its barrel. I will keep my rifle clean and ready, even as I am clean and ready. We will become part of each other. Before God I swear this creed. My rifle and I are the defenders of my country. We are the masters of our enemy. We are the saviors of my life. So be it, until victory is America's and there is no enemy."

U.S. Navy SEAL Training Program

FIRST PHASE (BASIC CONDITIONING), 8 WEEKS: Begins with four-mile timed runs in boots, timed obstacle courses, and two-mile ocean swims. The fourth week is known as "Hell Week," in which recruits undergo five and a half days of continuous running, swimming, boat drills, and lifting 500-pound logs, with no more than four hours' sleep in total. The ordeal commences just before midnight with an instructor waking trainees with machine-gun fire. The remaining four weeks are spent in the classroom.

SECOND PHASE (DIVING), 8 WEEKS: Qualifies recruits as basic combat swimmers.

THIRD PHASE (LAND WARFARE), 9 WEEKS: Trains candidates in weapons, demolition, and small unit tactics. Physical training becomes more strenuous as run distances increase and the passing times are lowered for the runs, swims, and obstacle course. The final three and a half weeks are spent on San Clemente Island, where recruits apply all the techniques they have learned.

The Agoge: Training Methods of the Ancient Spartans

Undertaken by boys from the age of seven.

1. Boys were forced to sleep naked in the middle of winter (and permitted only one layer of clothing during the day).
2. Boys were forbidden to wear shoes on long marches so as to strengthen the soles of their feet.
3. Meager rations. Boys were encouraged to supplement their diet by stealing extra food, though they were beaten severely if caught in the act.
4. The scourge. Boys were regularly whipped by their elders and taught to take pride in the degree of pain they could endure.

5. The cheese game was held annually in front of the altar of Orthia Artemis. Spartan boys had to run the gauntlet of older youths armed with sticks and whips and try, while still conscious, to retrieve wheels of cheese.
6. Periodic killing sprees in the countryside. The victims were Helot slaves working the land; each year "war" was declared on the Helots to keep them in line.
7. Pitched battles. Groups of boys were pitted against one another in free-for-alls of unarmed combat.
8. "Grinding the tree": A number of boys formed a line, with each pressing his shield against the boy in front of him with as much force as he could muster. The boy at the front of the line was ground against a tree until it toppled, a process often lasting several days and often with fatal results.
9. The "Oktonyktia" (eight nights): Twelve hundred warriors would march in full pack and armor for four nights, bivouacking during the day. During the next four days and nights they drilled almost continuously, breaking only for short rests. They ate half rations for the first four days, had no food for the next two, and no food or water for the last two days.

Iraq's Most Wanted

From the set of playing cards issued to U.S. troops during the 2003 Iraq War.

ACE OF SPADES: Saddam Hussein, Iraqi president
ACE OF HEARTS: Odai Hussein, Saddam's son
ACE OF DIAMONDS: Abid Hamid Mahmud, presidential secretary
ACE OF CLUBS: Qusai Hussein, Saddam's son
TWO JOKERS: One explains Arab titles and Iraqi surnames, the other Iraqi military ranks

Leaders Represented on Belgian Playing Cards during World War II

KING OF SPADES: Winston Churchill
KING OF DIAMONDS: Franklin D. Roosevelt
KING OF CLUBS: Charles de Gaulle
KING OF HEARTS: Joseph Stalin
JOKER: Adolf Hitler

The Chickenhawks

Defined as: Republicans who supported the 2003 war in Iraq after having avoided their own combat duty.

DICK CHENEY: Claimed to have "other priorities'" rather than serve in Vietnam.

RICHARD PERLE: Spent Vietnam enrolled at the University of Chicago.

RUSH LIMBAUGH: Avoided Vietnam due to anal cysts.

PAT ROBERTSON: Pulled out of Korea by his U.S. senator father as hostilities began.

JOHN ASHCROFT: Deferred his Vietnam tour of duty to teach business education.

BILL O'REILLY: Avoided Vietnam through a college deferment.

TRENT LOTT: A hardship exemption meant that he served as a college cheerleader instead.

TOM DELAY: Claimed he could not get into the army because it was too full of minorities to find room for him.

The Eight Wounds Sustained by Alexander the Great

Cleaver slash to the head
Sword blow to the thigh
Catapult missile in the chest

Arrow passed through the leg
Stone struck the head and neck
Dart pierced the shoulder
Arrow in the ankle
Arrow lodged in the lung

Animals at War

1. ELEPHANTS: The Carthaginians first used them against Rome at the siege of Agrigentum in 262 B.C., but the Romans famously learned to open ranks and simply let the beasts charge through. At the Battle of Panoramus in 251 B.C., the elephants were maddened with arrows into stampeding among their own lines, while at Zama in 202 B.C. they were scared away by trumpets. Elephants were also used extensively in India and in tenth-century China, where they were eventually abandoned as being too vulnerable to massed archery. At the siege of Qusu in China in 446, the attackers made bamboo lions, which frightened the city's elephants into trampling their fellow defenders.

2. DOGS: Red Army soldiers in World War II strapped bombs to dogs and attempted to destroy German tanks. However, the animals identified their own armies' vehicles with food and caused several Russian formations to retreat.

3. BATS: During World War II, the United States' Project X-Ray involved strapping miniature napalm charges to thousands of bats and releasing them over Japan. The plan was abandoned after the bats escaped and destroyed an aircraft hangar and a general's car in New Mexico.

4. CAMELS: Afghan mujahideen used kamikaze camels loaded with explosives against the Soviet occupation forces between 1979 and 1989. Camels were used as mobile water tankers during the march of Khalid bin al-Walid's Arab army from Iraq to Syria in 634. First they were forced to drink their fill before their mouths were bound

up to prevent them chewing the cud. They were then slaughtered as needed and the water drunk straight from their bellies.

5. RATS: The British Special Operations Executive used dummy rats packed with explosives to disable German munitions factories during World War II.

6. DOLPHINS: Both the Russian and U.S. navies have trained dolphins to locate mines.

7. SEA LIONS: Used by the U.S. Navy in the Persian Gulf to keep a lookout for enemy frogmen during the Iraq War of 2003.

8. TICKS: The U.S. Army attempted to use bloodsucking insects to detect hidden enemy troops, but their behavior proved too difficult to interpret.

9. PIGEONS: Americans trained these birds to ride in the noses of missiles and so guide them toward ships, though they have never been used in combat.

10. MONKEYS: In the *Arthashashtra* (Treatise on Siegecraft), the fourth-century B.C. Brahman chief minister Kautilya writes of burning out the defenders of strongholds by using trained monkeys to carry incendiary devices over the fortifications.

11. OXEN: At the siege of Jimo in 279 B.C., the defending commander Tian Dan of Qi sent out a hundred oxen dressed in silk costumes and with burning straw tied to their tails to make them look like dragons. The attackers fled.

12. PARROTS: During World War I, trained parrots were perched on the Eiffel Tower, from where they could give twenty minutes' warning of incoming aircraft. The practice was abandoned when it was discovered that the birds could not discriminate between German and Allied planes.

"The Art of Using Troops," from Sun Tzu's The Art of War

When ten to the enemy's one, surround him
When five times his strength, attack him

If double his strength, divide him
If equally matched you may engage him
If weaker numerically, be capable of withdrawing
And if in all respects unequal, be capable of eluding him,
for a small force is but booty for one more powerful.

Designations in the Dutch Resistance during the Nazi Occupation

"PRINCES": All who carried out acts of resistance
"PRIESTS": Harbor watchers and saboteurs
"BARRISTERS": Communications saboteurs
"BREWERS": Power-supply saboteurs
"PAINTERS": Railway saboteurs

Hollywood Rewrites

How military history has been changed to suit theater audiences and political ends

THEY DIED WITH THEIR BOOTS ON (1941): We are expected to believe that the genocidal American army commander George Armstrong Custer dies leaving a letter in which he defends the rights of Native Americans.

MISSION TO MOSCOW (1943): This Warner Brothers movie of life in America's wartime ally the Soviet Union excuses the purges and paints Stalin as the beneficent leader of a happy, prosperous country.

BATAAN (1943): Features a racially mixed platoon when none actually existed in the U.S. army.

OBJECTIVE BURMA! (1945): Errol Flynn is depicted as single-handedly clearing the Japanese out of Burma, with no mention of the British, Australian, and New Zealand forces that fought there. Winston Churchill was so enraged that the film was not released in Britain until 1952, accompanied by an apology.

THE ALAMO (1960): Director and star John Wayne decided that having his Davy Crockett run through by a Mexican lance before staggering to the powder room with a lit torch and blowing the fort to kingdom come was a better ending than surrendering to Santa Anna and being executed. Neither historically did Jim Bowie play a part in the fighting; he was bedridden with typhoid throughout.

SINK THE BISMARCK! (1960): The British take their revenge on Hollywood in a movie in which the Royal Navy hunts down and destroys the famous German battleship. In reality, the British were unable to find the *Bismarck,* which was sunk only after being spotted by a U.S. Navy pilot. However, faithful to British modesty, Royal Navy ships are shown being sunk that were not even hit in the battle, while numerous swordfish torpedo bombers are shot down when in fact all of them returned intact.

U-571 (2000): U.S. Navy sailors capture an Enigma code machine from a German U-boat, even though the actual raid was carried out by the British in 1941, before America had even entered the war.

THE PATRIOT (2000): Depicts the English locking up hundreds of women and children in a church and then setting fire to it. Nothing resembling this crime was committed by either side in the American Revolutionary War, the event being taken from a Nazi atrocity at Oradour-sur-Glane in France in 1944.

Hollywood Heroes

War records of the stars.

CHARLES BRONSON: Nose gunner in bombers, flying twenty-one combat missions.

DOUGLAS FAIRBANKS JR.: Joined the naval reserves before World War II, during which he served on a battleship and as a commando sent on shore assaults. He later helped organize the precursors to the Navy SEALs and retired as a captain.

ED WOOD: The B-movie director and former U.S. Marine claimed to have once taken part in a military landing wearing a bra and panties under his Marine uniform.

GLENN FORD: The only actor ever to serve with both the Green Berets and the French Foreign Legion.

CLARK GABLE: Although overage, he enlisted as a private in the U.S. Army Air Corps in 1942, attended Officers' Candidate School, and graduated as a second lieutenant. He then flew aboard B-17 bomber missions over Europe to obtain combat footage for the movies.

LEE MARVIN: Assaulted twenty-one beaches as a U.S. Marine and was wounded in the Battle of Saipan.

JACK PALANCE: Required facial reconstruction from terrible injuries received in 1943 when his B-17 crash-landed.

RONALD REAGAN: A captain in the U.S. Army Air Corps, he was not allowed to fly due to hearing problems and spent the war appearing in training films.

ROD STEIGER: Falsified his age to enlist at sixteen and served as a torpedo man in the U.S. Navy.

HUMPHREY BOGART: Wounded in World War I; tried to enlist in World War II but was turned down because of his age.

AUDREY HEPBURN: Worked as a courier for World War II resistance fighters in Holland when she was a child.

JAMES STEWART: Flew twenty-five combat missions in a B-17 and won the Distinguished Flying Cross.

ELI WALLACH: Served as a sergeant in the U.S. Army Medical Corps as an administrative clerk.

KIRK DOUGLAS: Served as a communications officer on a submarine, and was injured by a depth charge that struck his patrol vessel.

HARRISON FORD: Applied for conscientious objector status during the Vietnam War. He was willing to undertake alternative service but it was never required of him.

SYLVESTER STALLONE: The Rambo actor managed to avoid military service in Vietnam and spent 1965 to 1967 as an athletic coach at a girls' school in France.

Famous 4-Fs—Unfit for Active Service

Phil Silvers—poor eyesight (he later remarked that couldn't "see" himself fighting a war)

Frank Sinatra—perforated eardrum

John Wayne—perforated eardrum

Gary Cooper—displaced hip

Errol Flynn—heart condition

Marlon Brando—knee injury sustained in high school football

Jackie Gleason—overweight

Richard Widmark—perforated eardrum

Dean Martin—hernia

Danny Kaye—bad back

Superman—"blind as a bat." According to the comic book, the man of steel failed the enlistment medical because he accidentally read the eye-test card in the next room and was thus branded.

War Records of the Superheroes

How comic book characters spent World War II.

1. SUPERMAN: Demolished the Siegfried line before arresting Hitler in the Eagle's Nest and flying him to Geneva to face trial for war crimes. Superman also picked up Stalin from the Kremlin in a brief detour.

2. BATMAN: Spent the war in counterintelligence, foiling Axis plots against America and Great Britain, such as a Japanese plan to turn U.S. citizens into a zombie legion.

3. THE GREEN LANTERN AND THE FLASH: Worked in England for counterintelligence.

4. CAPTAIN AMERICA: Joined the army disguised as a private and went on to punch Adolf Hitler in the face.

Swiss Neutrality

**The Alpine Nation's Ambivalent Contribution
to the Second World War.**

1. Switzerland shot down several German aircraft. Hermann Göring sent a sabotage team in revenge, but it was captured before it could destroy the Swiss air force on the ground.

2. The Swiss tried but failed to destroy Allied bombers on their way to Germany.

3. Blackout conditions were implemented in their cities to prevent Allied bombers from navigating their way to Germany by their lights. This resulted in the accidental bombing of Swiss cities, for which the U.S. government later paid $62 in compensation.

4. Both the communist party and the fascist movement were banned in 1940.

5. Coal and steel were carried between Germany and Italy via Swiss railways.

7. Swiss territory functioned as "home base" for escaped Allied POWs and safe ground for French and Italian resistance fighters.

8. Switzerland gave transit to 400,000 refugees over the course of the war, though its borders were closed in 1942 when Vichy France declared 170,000 Jews to be undesirable residents.

9. A total of 187 Swiss spies were captured by the Germans, 17 of whom were executed.

10. Swiss banks laundered hundreds of millions of dollars' worth of gold that the Nazis had stolen from Jewish victims of the Holocaust.

Sympathy for the Devil

Noncombatant countries that flew flags at half-mast after Hitler's suicide in April 1945:

> The Republic of Ireland (Eire)
> Portugal

The Nuremberg Trials

The following Nazis, with their convictions and punishments, were accused of the crimes "conspiracy" (C), "crimes against peace" (CP), "war crimes" (WC), and "crimes against humanity" (CH).

Hermann Göring	C, CP, WC, CH	Hanging*
Rudolf Hess	C, CP	Life imprisonment
Joachim von Ribbentrop	C, CP, WC, CH	Hanging
Wilhelm Keitel	C, CP, WC, CH	Hanging
Ernst Kaltenbrunner	WC, CH	Hanging
Alfred Rosenberg	C, CP, WC, CH	Hanging
Hans Frank	WC, CH	Hanging
Wilhelm Frick	CP, WC, CH	Hanging
Julius Streicher	CH	Hanging
Walther Funk	CP, WC, CH	Life imprisonment
Hjalmar Schacht		Acquitted
Karl Dönitz	CP, WC	10 years
Erich Raeder	C, CP, WC	Life imprisonment
Baldur von Schirach	CH	20 years
Fritz Sauckel	WC, CH	Hanging

Alfred Jodl	C, CP, WC, CH	Hanging
Martin Bormann	WC, CH	Hanging†
Franz von Papen		Acquitted
Artur Seyss-Inquart	CP, WC, CH	Hanging
Albert Speer	WC, CH	20 years
Konstantin von Neurath	C, CP, WC, CH	15 years
Hans Fritzsche		Acquitted

*Committed suicide before the sentence could be carried out
† Tried in absentia

Other would-be defendants were Hitler, Himmler, Goebbels, Robert Ley, who had already committed suicide, and Gustav Krupp, who was declared unfit to stand trial.

Famous Commanders' Nicknames

THOMAS J. JACKSON: "Stonewall" Jackson, because at the Battle of Bull Run, General Barnard Bee shouted to his men, "Look! There's Jackson, standing like a stone wall. Rally behind him!" While at the Virginia Military Institute Jackson was also called "Square Box" for his unusually large feet, "Old Jack" for his eccentricities, and "Tom Fool" for his poor teaching abilities.

WILLIAM L. JACKSON: "Mudwall," in deference to his more famous cousin.

GEORGE ARMSTRONG CUSTER: "Curly," for his locks of blond hair. Curly was also the nickname of Custer's nemesis, Crazy Horse.

WILLIAM E. JONES: "Grumble," due to his constant complaining.

GEORGE B. MCCLELLAN: "Little Napoleon," "Little Mac," and, due to the slow but steady pace of his advances, "The Virginia Creeper."

ULYSSES S. GRANT: "Unconditional Surrender" Grant, somewhat inaccurately, for his refusal to compromise.

JAMES STUART: "Jeb" Stuart, for his first three initials, J. E. B. (James Ewell Brown)

WINFIELD SCOTT: "Old Fuss and Feathers," because obesity and gout eventually rendered him unable to ride a horse for any length of time

JOHN J. PERSHING: "Black Jack," for his high regard for black soldiers.

WILLIAM F. HALSEY: "Bull" Halsey and "Fighting" Halsey, because of his enthusiasm for attacking.

GEORGE S. PATTON: "Blood and Guts," for belligerence that bordered on the psychopathic.

JOSEPH W. STILWELL: "Vinegar" Joe, for his forcefully expressed opinions.

DOUGLAS MACARTHUR: "Dug-out Doug," because he spent so much time underground in the fortress on Corregidor holding out against the Japanese.

OMAR BRADLEY: "The GI General," for his respect among the lower ranks.

MARK CLARK: "The American Eagle," bestowed by Sir Winston Churchill for his fighting qualities and possibly also for his large, hooked nose.

H. NORMAN SCHWARZKOPF: "Stormin'" Norman, for the speed and magnitude of his invasion of Kuwait.

How They Spent Their Retirement

Late-life pastimes and occupations of former military commanders.

LEWIS WALLACE: Wrote the novel *Ben Hur*.

GEORGE B. McCLELLAN: Chief engineer of the New York Department of Docks, before becoming governor of New Jersey.

NATHAN BEDFORD FORREST: Became the first grand wizard of the Ku Klux Klan.

PIERRE G. T. BEAUREGARD: Managed the Louisiana state lottery.

ALBERT PIKE: Became the highest-ranking freemason in the United States.

PHILIP SHERIDAN: The destroyer of the Shenandoah Valley became the protector of Yellowstone National Park.

GERONIMO: Converted to Christianity and became a farmer.

SITTING BULL: Traveled with Buffalo Bill Cody and his Wild West Show.

JOHN J. PERSHING: Won the 1932 Pulitzer Prize in history for his memoir, *My Experiences in the World War*.

JAMES H. DOOLITTLE: Oil executive.

Native American Chiefs and Heroes

BLACK HAWK (1767–1838): War chief of the Sauk who resented the displacement of his Spanish friends by American settlers. Fought with the British during the War of 1812 before declaring war on the U.S. government in 1832. Later that year his forces were almost wiped out by U.S. troops.

COCHISE (C.1812–74): Chiracahua Apache chief whose response to a false accusation of kidnapping led to an eleven-year war against the U.S. government.

CHIEF JOSEPH (C.1840–1904): Nez Percé chief who led his forces successfully against superior odds in 1877 before his final surrender with the words "I will fight no more forever."

GERONIMO (1829–1909): Apache war chief who led raids in Mexico and the United States after his mother, wife, and children were murdered by Mexicans.

RED CLOUD (1822–1909): Sioux chief who fought bloodily to discourage white settlement in Wyoming.

SITTING BULL (C.1831–90): Sioux victor at the Battle of the Little Bighorn in 1876.

TECUMSEH (1768–1813): Shawnee chief who formed a confederacy of tribes to resist U.S. settler encroachment in the American Midwest, later fighting for the British as a general in the War of 1812.

West Point Class Position of Famous Commanders

ROBERT E. LEE: 1829, 2nd out of 46
WILLIAM TECUMSEH SHERMAN: 1840, 6th out of 42
ULYSSES S. GRANT: 1843, 21st out of 39
GEORGE E. PICKETT: 1846, 59th out of 59
GEORGE B. MCCLELLAN: 1846, 2nd out of 59
GEORGE ARMSTRONG CUSTER: 1861, 35th out of 35
JOHN J. PERSHING: 1896, 30th out of 77
DOUGLAS MACARTHUR: 1903, 1st out of 93
GEORGE S. PATTON: 1909, 46th out of 103
DWIGHT D. EISENHOWER: 1915, 61st out of 168
OMAR BRADLEY: 1915, 44th out of 168
WILLIAM C. WESTMORELAND: 1936, 112th out of 276
ALEXANDER HAIG: 1947, 167th out of 363
WESLEY CLARK: 1966, 1st out of 579

West Point Dropouts

EDGAR ALLAN POE: The writer was expelled in 1831 for "gross neglect of duty" and "disobedience of orders."
JAMES MCNEILL WHISTLER: Judged "deficient in chemistry" as a student and expelled in 1854; he proved a far better painter.
TIMOTHY LEARY: The future LSD guru dropped out in 1941.

Gods and Goddesses of War

ARES: Ancient Greek
MARS: Roman
CAMULUS: Celtic
ANUKE: Ancient Egyptian
SKANDA: Hindu

WURUKATTE: Hittite
HUITZILOPOCHTLI: Aztec
NACON: Mayan
ASHURE: Assyrian
TYR: Norse/Germanic
KORRAWI: Tamil
ARAY: Armenian
HADUR: Hungarian (Hunnic)
LARAN: Etruscan
ERRA: Sumerian
HACHIMAN: Japanese
CHUN-T'I: Chinese

Special Forces by Country

AUSTRALIA: Australian Special Air Service Regiment (SASR)
BELGIUM: Equipes Spécialisées de Reconnaissance (ESR)
CANADA: Joint Task Force Two
DENMARK: JaegerKorpset (Ranger Corps)
EGYPT: Task Force 777
FRANCE: Régiment parachutiste d'infanterie de marine (RIPMa)
GERMANY: Kommando Spezialkräfte (KSK) (Combat Diver
    Company), Grenzschutzgruppe (GSG-9) (Border Police Force)
ISRAEL: Sayaret Golani (Golani Reconnaissance Company)
ITALY: Commando Raggruppamento Subacqui ed Incursioni
    (COMSUBIN)
MEXICO: Force F "Zorros"
NETHERLANDS: Bizondere Bijstands Eenheid (BBE) (Special
    Backup Unit)
NORWAY: Marine Jagerne (Marine Hunters)
REPUBLIC OF IRELAND: Sciathan Fianoglach an Airm (Army
    Rangers Wing)
RUSSIA: Spetsnaz
SOUTH AFRICA: 1 Reconnaissance Commando

UK: Special Air Service (SAS), Special Boat Service (SBS)
USA: Delta Force, Navy SEALs, Green Berets (U.S. Army
Special Forces)

Military Bureaucracy

Memo from the Alaska Air Command, February 1973.

Due to an administrative error, the original of the attached letter
was forwarded to you. A new original has been accomplished and
forwarded to AAC/JA (Alaskan Air Command, Judge Advocate
office). Please place this carbon copy in your files and destroy the
original.

**Letter Allegedly Written by the Duke of Wellington to
the British Foreign Office in London from Central Spain,
August 1812.**

Gentlemen,

Whilst marching from Portugal to a position which com-
mands the approach to Madrid and the French forces, my
officers have been diligently complying with your requests
which have been sent by H.M. ship from London to Lisbon
and thence by dispatch to our headquarters.

We have enumerated our saddles, bridles, tents and tent
poles, and all manner of sundry items for which His Majesty's
Government holds me accountable. I have dispatched reports
on the character, wit, and spleen of every officer. Each item
and every farthing has been accounted for, with two regrettable
exceptions for which I beg your indulgence.

Unfortunately the sum of one shilling and ninepence remains unaccounted for in one infantry battalion's petty cash

and there has been a hideous confusion as to the number of jars of raspberry jam issued to one cavalry regiment during a sandstorm in western Spain. This reprehensible carelessness may be related to the pressure of circumstance, since we are at war with France, a fact which may come as something of a surprise to you gentlemen in Whitehall.

This brings me to my present purpose, which is to request elucidation of my instructions from His Majesty's Government so that I may better understand why I am dragging an army over these barren plains. I construe that perforce it must be one of two alternative duties, as given below. I shall pursue either one with the best of my ability, but I cannot do both:

1. To train an army of uniformed British clerks in Spain for the benefit of the accountants and copy-boys in London or perchance,
2. To see to it that the forces of Napoleon are driven out of Spain.

Your most obedient servant,
Wellington

Officer Fitness Reports

Excerpts supposedly from British Royal Navy and Royal Marines evaluation forms but widely circulated via e-mail, with varying attributions.

1. His men would follow him anywhere, but only out of curiosity.
2. I would not breed from this officer.
3. When she opens her mouth, it seems that this is only to change whichever foot was previously in there.
4. He has carried out each and every one of his duties to his entire satisfaction.

5. This young lady has delusions of adequacy.
6. Since my last report, he has reached rock bottom and has started to dig.
7. She sets low personal standards and then consistently fails to achieve them.
8. This officer should go far, and the sooner he starts, the better.
9. Works well when under constant supervision and cornered like a rat in a trap.
10. This man is depriving a village somewhere of an idiot.

The World's Largest Land Armies

1. China—1,700,000*
2. India—1,200,000
3. North Korea—900,000*
4. South Korea—560,000*
5. Pakistan—520,000
6. USA—475,000
7. Iraq—360,00†
8. Myanmar—325,000
9. Russia—320,000
10. Iran—320,000*

*Includes conscripts
†Pre-2003

The World's Largest Air Forces

By number of combat jets.

1. Russia—3,996
2. China—3,520
3. United States—2,598
4. India—774

5. Taiwan—598
6. North Korea—593
7. Egypt—583
8. France—531
9. Ukraine—521
10. South Korea—488

The World's Largest Navies

By personnel.

1. United States—369,800
2. China—230,000
3. Russia—171,500
4. Taiwan—68,000
5. France—62,600
6. South Korea—60,000
7. India—53,000
8. Turkey—51,000
9. Indonesia—47,000
10. North Korea—46,000

The World's Largest Military Budgets, 2003

1. United States—$334 billion
2. Russia—$60 billion
3. China—$55 billion
4. France—$47 billion
5. Japan—$41 billion
6. Germany—$39 billion
7. UK—$33 billion
8. Italy—$20 billion
9. Saudi Arabia—$18 billion
10. Brazil—$13.4 billion
11. South Korea—$13 billion
12. India—$12 billion
13. Iran—$10 billion
14. Australia—$9.3 billion
15. Israel—$9 billion
16. Spain—$8.6 billion
17. Turkey—$8 billion
18. Canada—$8 billion

19. Netherlands—$7 billion
20. Greece—$6 billion
21. North Korea—$5 billion
22. Singapore—$4.5 billion
23. Sweden—$4.4 billion
24. Argentina—$4.3 billion
25. Egypt—$4 billion
26. Mexico—$4 billion
27. Poland—$3.5 billion
28. Colombia—$3.3 billion
29. Norway—$3 billion
30. Belgium—$3 billion
31. Pakistan—$2.5 billion
32. Switzerland—$2.5 billion
33. Denmark—$2.5 billion
34. Oman—$2.4 billion
35. Kuwait—$2 billion
36. Algeria—$1.9 billion
37. South Africa—$1.8 billion
38. Finland—$1.8 billion
39. Thailand—$1.7 billion
40. Malaysia—$1.7 billion
41. Morocco—$1.4 billion
42. Libya—$1.3 billion
43. Iraq—$1.3 billion
44. Portugal—$1.3 billion
45. Czech Republic—$1.2 billion
46. Angola—$1.2 billion
47. Hungary—$1.1 billion
48. Syria—$1 billion
49. Peru—$1 billion
50. Romania—$1 billion

*Iraq pre–Iraq War

Items in U.S. Military Audit 2000/2001

$45,000 for luxury cruises

$38,000 for lap dancing at strip clubs near military bases

$24,000 for a sofa and armchair

$16,000 for a corporate golf membership

$9,800 for Halloween costumes

$7,373 for closing costs on a home

$4,600 for white beach sand and $19,000 worth of decorative "river rock" at a military base in the Arabian desert

$3,400 for a Sumo wrestling suit

$1,800 for executive pillows

Developments in Weapons Technology

Their cultural origins.

c. 3500 B.C. chariot—Sumerians
c. 3000 B.C. bronze—Assyrians
c. 1500 B.C. wrought iron—Hittites
c. 650 B.C. trireme—Greeks
c. 300 B.C. steel—India
c. 200 chainmail armor—Romans
c. 300 stirrup—China
672 Greek fire—Byzantines
1100 crossbow (fully mechanized version)—France
1160 longbow—England
c. 1200 gunpowder (weaponized)—China
c. 1250 rockets (weaponized)—China
c. 1350 firearms—France
1451 mortar—Ottomans
1592 armored warship—Korea
1718 machine gun—England
1776 submarine—American colonies
1776 sea mine—American colonies
1797 parachute—France
1866 torpedo—England
1866 dynamite—Sweden
1874 barbed wire—United States
1902 submarine periscope—United States
1903 airplane—United States
1915 poison gas—Germany
1915 depth charge—United Kingdom
1916 tank—United Kingdom
1918 aircraft carrier*—United Kingdom
1918 sonar—France
1933 radar—United Kingdom

1937 helicopter—Germany
1939 jet aircraft—United Kingdom
1942 napalm—United States
1943 night-vision equipment—Germany
1943 guided missile—Germany
1945 A-bomb—United States
1953 H-bomb—United States
1955 nuclear submarine—United States
1968 antiballistic missile†—U.S.S.R.
1977 neutron bomb—United States
1982 stealth aircraft—United States

*In 1918 the Royal Navy launched HMS *Argus*. HMS *Furious* had been adapted for the purpose in 1917.

†The Soviet Galosh system was deployed in 1968 for the defense of Moscow from nuclear attack. Its warheads were themselves nuclear and it is unknown how much protection they might have afforded the city's populace.

Naval Watches

12 NOON TO 4:00 P.M.: Afternoon watch
4:00 P.M. TO 6:00 P.M.: First dogwatch
6:00 P.M. TO 8:00 P.M.: Second dogwatch
8:00 P.M. TO MIDNIGHT: First night watch
MIDNIGHT TO 4:00 A.M.: Middle or mid watch
4:00 A.M. TO 8:00 A.M.: Morning watch
8:00 A.M. TO 12 NOON: Forenoon watch

Leonardo da Vinci's Ideas for Weapons

1. A tank powered by horses or men with hand cranks
2. Submarine
3. One-man battleship

4. A giant cog for sweeping away attackers trying to climb fortifications
5. Lightweight portable bridges
6. Catapult missiles with gunpowder warheads and stabilizing fins
7. A ballista (giant crossbow) 76 feet long
8. Breech-loading, water-cooled cannons
9. Antipersonnel cannonballs that shatter upon impact
10. The wheel-lock firing mechanism (used centuries later to improve on the matchlock)
11. A chariot with rotating scythes
12. Double-hulled fighting ships
13. Helicopter

Volunteers for the International Brigade during the Spanish Civil War 1936–39

1. France, 10,000
2. Germany, 5,000
3. Poland, 4,000
4. Italy, 3,500
5. Britain, 2,500
6. United States, 2,500
7. Belgium, 1,700
8. Czechoslovakia, 1,500
9. Yugoslavia, 1,200
10. Latin America, 1,000
11. Canada, 1,000
12. Hungary, 1,000
13. Scandinavia, 1,000
14. Holland, 600
15. Switzerland, 400

The Coalition of the Willing

The thirty nations named by Colin Powell as allies in the Iraq War of 2003.

AFGHANISTAN: 0 troops sent
ALBANIA: 70 troops
AUSTRALIA: 2,000 troops
AZERBAIJAN: 0 troops
BULGARIA: 150 nuclear, biological, and chemical (NBC)
    decontamination experts
COLOMBIA: 0 troops
CZECH REPUBLIC: 1 NBC team
DENMARK: 1 submarine, 1 warship
EL SALVADOR: 0 troops
ERITREA: 0 troops
ESTONIA: 0 troops
ETHIOPIA: 0 troops
GEORGIA: 0 troops
HUNGARY: 0 troops
ITALY: 0 troops
JAPAN: 0 troops
SOUTH KOREA: 0 troops
LATVIA: Undisclosed
LITHUANIA: 0 troops
MACEDONIA: 0 troops
NETHERLANDS: 360 troops
NICARAGUA: 0 troops
PHILIPPINES: Undisclosed
POLAND: 270 noncombat troops
ROMANIA: 278 NBC experts
SLOVAKIA: 0 troops
SPAIN: 1 medical ship
TURKEY: 0 troops

UNITED KINGDOM: 45,000 troops
UZBEKISTAN: 0 troops

This coalition was later joined by: Costa Rica, Dominican Republic, Honduras, Iceland, Marshall Islands, Micronesia, Mongolia, Palau, Rwanda, the Solomon Islands, Tonga, Uganda, and the Ukraine, none of whom sent troops.

The "Free World Military Forces"

U.S.-allied troops in the Vietnam War.

1. Koreans: 48,869
2. Thais: 11,568
3. Australians: 7,672
4. Canadians: 1,200 (did not fight under the FWMF banner)
5. New Zealanders: 552
6. Filipinos: 552
7. Taiwanese: 29
8. Spaniards: 10

American troops totaled some 5,720,000.

German U-Boat Aces of the Second World War

Commander	Ships	Tonnage sunk
Otto Kretschmer	47	274,386
Wolfgang Lüth	47	225,756
Erich Topp	36	198,658
Günther Prien	30	186,253
Heinrich Liebe	34	185,377
Heinrich Lehmann-Willenbrock	25	179,212
Viktor Schütze	34	174,896
Herbert Schultze	26	169,709
Karl-Friedrich Merten	27	167,271
Joachim Schepke	38	161,340

Fastest Fighter Aircraft of the Second World War

Aircraft	Country	Speed
Messerschmitt Me 163	Germany	596 mph
Messerschmitt Me 262	Germany	560 mph
Heinkel He 162A	Germany	522 mph
North American P-51H Mustang	United States	487 mph
Focke-Wulf Ta 152H	Germany	472 mph
Republic P-47N Thunderbolt	United States	467 mph
Lavochkin La-11	U.S.S.R.	460 mph
Vickers Supermarine Spitfire XIV	Great Britain	448 mph
Yakovlev Yak-3	U.S.S.R.	447 mph
Focke-Wulf Fw 190D	Germany	435 mph

Fastest Postwar Production Fighter Aircraft

Aircraft	Country	Speed
Mikoyan-Gurevich MiG-25 Foxbat	U.S.S.R.	2,110 mph (Mach 3.2)
McDonnell Douglas F-15 Eagle	United States	1,650 mph (Mach 2.5)
Grumman F-14 Tomcat	United States	1,565 mph (Mach 2.37)
Mikoyan-Gurevich (MiG-23 Flogger)	U.S.S.R.	1,555 mph (Mach 2.35)
Sukhoi Su-27 Flanker	U.S.S.R.	1,555 mph (Mach 2.35)
Mikoyan-Gurevich MiG-29 Fulcrum	U.S.S.R.	1,520 mph (Mach 2.3)
Israel Industries IAI F-21 Kfir	Israel	1,520 mph (Mach 2.3)
English Electric Lightning F 6	Britain	1,500 mph (Mach 2.3)
Shenyang J-8 Finback	China	1,450 mph (Mach 2.2)
Dassault Mirage 2000	France	1,450 mph (Mach 2.2)
Panavia F Mk 3 Tornado	Great Britain	1,450 mph (Mach 2.2)

Abandon Ship!

Scuttled fleets.

1. THE CONQUISTADORES: In 1519, Hernán Cortés sailed from Cuba to conquer the Aztec empire of Mexico by 1521 with a fleet of eleven ships. After landing he built a fort at Veracruz, then scuttled his fleet to prevent desertions and show his men that there could be no turning back.

2. THE POTOMAC ARMADA: John Murray, Earl of Dunmore and the last British governor of Virginia, entered the Potomac in 1776 with seventy-two ships. Anchoring at St. George Island to take on provisions, his forces were depleted by smallpox and attacks from revolutionary troops. After two weeks the earl decided to scuttle and burn most of his ships and escape with the remainder.

3. THE BLACK SEA FLEET: In 1854, during the Crimean War, the Russians scuttled their fleet to attempt to block off the harbor entrance to Sebastopol rather than fight the British force at sea.

4. THE HIGH SEAS FLEET: At the end of World War I, most of the German Imperial Navy was sent to Scapa Flow with skeleton crews as a gesture of good faith while armistice talks were conducted. Fearing that the British would board and steal the ships, the German commander, Rear Admiral von Reuter, ordered the scuttling of the fleet in June 1919. All but eight ships out of seventy-four were later refloated.

5. THE FRENCH NAVY: After their decision to occupy Vichy France in 1942, the Germans mined the harbor mouth at Toulon to prevent the escape of the rump French fleet to North Africa. Crewmen and Free French supporters scuttled their vessels to prevent their capture.

6. U-BOATS: On April 30, 1945, Germany's Admiral Dönitz issued an order code-named Regenbogen for the scuttling of almost the entire fleet in order to preserve the honor of the Kriegs-

marine. The Allies forced him to cancel the order, but the U-boat commanders in the western Baltic went ahead anyway, sending 232 submarines to the seabed.

A Short History of Biological Warfare

1. POISONED WELLS: In the sixth century B.C., the Assyrians poisoned enemy wells with rye ergot, while Solon of Athens used the purgative herb hellebore (skunk cabbage) to poison the water supply during his siege of Krissa. In the fourth century B.C., the Greeks contaminated their enemies' wells with animal corpses, while at the Battle of Tortona, Italy, in 1155, Barbarossa used human corpses to pollute the enemy water supply.

2. POISON ARROWS: In the fifth century B.C., Scythian archers dipped their arrows in animal dung so that the wounds they caused would become infected.

3. THE PLAGUE: In 1346–47, the Muslim Tatar De Mussis caused an epidemic of bubonic plague in Caffa on Russia's Black Sea in the Crimea by catapulting infected corpses over the city walls. At the siege of La Calle in 1785, Tunisian troops threw plague-ridden clothing into the city. In 1940, a plague epidemic in China and Manchuria followed reported overflights by Japanese planes dropping plague-infected fleas.

4. MANURE AND CORPSES: During the siege of Karlstejn in the Holy Roman Empire in 1422, dead soldiers and 2,000 cartloads of manure were catapulted over the fortifications.

5. VINTAGE LEPROSY: In 1485 near Naples, the Spanish supplied the French with wine laced with lepers' blood.

6. SMALLPOX: In 1763, during the French and Indian War, British colonel Henry Bouquet gave smallpox-infected blankets to the Indians at Fort Pitt, in Pennsylvania, resulting in an epidemic.

7. ANTHRAX: During World War I, the Germans infected nearly 5,000 mules and horses in Mesopotamia and sent anthrax to

Romania to infect sheep being transported to Russia. Four people died in 2001 when the U.S. postal system was used to distribute spores.

Ill-Treatment of Prisoners

1. THE BATTLE OF AEGOSPOTAMI, 405 B.C.: After Lysander's Spartan fleet had defeated the Athenians, 3,000 to 4,000 prisoners were executed.

2. THE BATTLE OF CHANGPING, 260 B.C.: 400,000 survivors from the Chinese state of Zhao's 450,000-strong army surrendered to the Qin general Bo Qi. Every last man was put to death.

3. SPENDIUS AND AUTITARIUS: The commanders of the mercenary revolt against Carthage surrendered with 40,000 starving troops in 238 B.C. Spendius was crucified and his men were slaughtered.

4. SPARTACUS: After Marcus Licinius Crassus put down the slave revolt of Spartacus in 71 B.C., the Romans crucified 6,000 captured slaves along the Appian Way as a warning to others.

5. THE BATTLE OF BALATHISTA, 1014: The victorious Byzantine emperor Basil II blinded his 15,000 Bulgar prisoners, leaving one man in every hundred with one good eye so that he could lead his comrades home.

6. MERCADIER: Richard the Lionheart's dying wish in 1199 was that the crossbowman who had shot him should be spared and given a sum of money. Richard's mercenary captain Mercadier instead had the man flayed alive and impaled.

7. THE BATTLE OF AGINCOURT, 1415: Several thousand French prisoners were allegedly executed on the spot at the orders of English King Henry V so that he could redeploy the soldiers guarding them.

8. THE BRIDGE OVER THE RIVER KWAI: The Thai-Burma Railway was completed in 1943 by 68,000 Allied POWs and 200,000 Asian slaves. Due to the cruelty of their Japanese overseers, 18,000 POWs and 78,000 Asians died in the process.

9. THE SURVIVORS OF STALINGRAD: Of the 90,000 Germans of Field Marshal von Paulus's Sixth Army who surrendered at the city in 1943, only 5,000 returned from the Soviet Union alive, most having spent ten years in captivity.

10. THE NAZIS: An estimated 3 million to 4 million Soviet POWs died at German hands from murder, maltreatment, exposure, and starvation. Also, after Italy's surrender to the Allies in 1943, 4,750 Italian soldiers were executed by the Germans in Cephalonia.

11. THE KATYŃ MASSACRE: More than 180,000 Polish POWs fell into Soviet hands when their country was partitioned by Germany in 1939. Some 4,400 officers had their hands tied with wire before they were shot in the back of the head and dumped in a mass grave. Soviet authorities initially blamed the atrocity on the Nazis before finally admitting guilt in 1990.

12. THE VIET CONG: During the Vietnam War, American POWs were routinely beaten, starved, tortured, politically indoctrinated, and sometimes executed by their VC captors.

A POW's Statement, by Vice Admiral James B. Stockdale

Ten years ago [1963], I toured the Old Yuma Territorial Prison with my two eldest sons, ages 12 and 8. Their boyish reactions to the filthy cells used for solitary confinement were predictable. A blend of wonderment and horror crossed their faces as they peered in at leg irons in the tiny, windowless concrete boxes. I assured the boys that the days of old Western desperadoes, as well as jails like these, were gone forever.

Little did I know that within a few years I would find myself in an old French-built isolated cellblock in Hanoi. This jail we called Alcatraz. I was one of eleven Americans living in tiny windowless boxes (complete with leg irons) finding out firsthand the capabilities of the human spirit in such as situation. Pedantic arguments of international politics were wasted on us. We had a war to fight and were committed to fighting it from lonely concrete boxes. Our very fiber and sinew were the only weapons at our disposal. Each man's values from his own private sources provided the strength enabling him to maintain his sense of purpose and dedication. They placed unity above self. Self-indulgence was a luxury that could not be afforded.

Each member of our "Alcatraz gang" fought his war from a filthy cell. All but one of us, Ron Storz, came home alive. Ron was a tiger to the end. For us he will always remain a symbol of courage, fidelity and dedication.

Military Etymology

AMMUNITION: From the French *munition* (all war essentials).

BAZOOKA: From its supposed resemblance to the bazoo or kazoo.

BOMB: From the Greek *bombos* (boom).

BULLET: From the French *boule* (ball)—any projectile (cannon or musket).

CHINDIT: A corruption of Chinthé, the name of a mythical Burmese beast, half-lion and half-dragon.

COMMANDO: From the Portuguese word meaning "command," which the Boers in South Africa used to identify local militia units.

GRENADE: From the Latin *granatus* (seed-filled).

GUERRILLA: From the Spanish for "little war," referring to resisters of the French occupation during the Peninsular War of 1808–14.

GUN: From the Old Norse Gunnhildr (a woman's name).

MISSILE: From the Latin *missilis* (a thrown or fired weapon).

PARTISAN: From the French word *partis,* used to mean foraging parties.

TANK: The first examples were sent to the Western Front in containers marked "Petrogrand" for secrecy, the cover story being that these were water tanks being developed for the Russians.

TATTOO: A Thirty Years' War corruption of the "taps" that were used to plug wine barrels at the end of a drinking session.

TECHNICALS: Pickup trucks with mounted machine guns were given this name during the war in Somalia in 1991–95 by journalists who hired them for protection while filing claims for "technical" expenses.

Cold War Doctrines

TRUMAN DOCTRINE: The commitment to contain the communist threat to the world within its 1948 borders.

EISENHOWER DOCTRINE: The commitment to send U.S. troops to the Middle East to counter any communist threat.

FORMOSA DOCTRINE: American resolve to protect Taiwan from Chinese communist aggression.

MASSIVE RETALIATION: Policy of responding to a Soviet attack on NATO with nuclear weapons.

NUCLEAR DETERRENCE: The notion that the possession of nuclear weapons alone is enough to prevent foreign invasion.

REAGAN DOCTRINE: Military aid to anticommunist insurgents in the Third World.

MUTUALLY ASSURED DESTRUCTION (MAD): The excuse for new weapons development on the grounds that the systems created by both sides would be able to destroy the enemy even if one's own country were already destroyed, thereby preventing a "first strike" by either side.

DOMINO THEORY: The opinion of U.S. president Lyndon Johnson's advisers that if South Vietnam fell to the communists, the same fate would befall other Asian countries and then countries outside of Asia.

BREZHNEV DOCTRINE: Soviet policy of invading Warsaw Pact allies if they moved too far away from orthodox Soviet communism, as did Czechoslovakia in 1968.

Napoleon's Medical Problems (Real and Exaggerated)

1. COLIC: When the pain subsided he sometimes had to sleep during battles.
2. PEPTIC ULCERS.
3. DYSURIA: Making it painful for him to pass urine.
4. PITUITARY DYSPLASIA: Stunted his growth.
5. OEDEMA OF THE CHEST: Excess fluid in the lungs, giving him a persistent cough.
6. FEVERS.
7. CONSTIPATION: From childhood onward.
8. CHRONIC GASTROENTERITIS (when not constipated).
9. PROLAPSED HEMORRHOIDS (alleged): Eventually making it impossible for him to mount his horse at Waterloo.
10. MICRO-PENIS: One inch long and resembling a grape; supposedly the dictator's organ was cut off at autopsy and eventually put up for auction by Christie's in 1972, where it failed to reach the reserve price.

The "Black Book"

Writers on the Gestapo hit list should Great Britain have become occupied by the Nazis.

1. Vera Brittain
2. Noël Coward
3. Sigmund Freud (died September 23, 1939)
4. Aldous Huxley

5. J. B. Priestley
6. Bertrand Russell
7. C. P. Snow
8. Stephen Spender
9. Lytton Strachey (died January 21, 1932)
10. Rebecca West
11. Virginia Woolf

Second World War Fighter and Bomber Production

Aircraft	Country	Units
Ilyushin Il-2 Shturmovik	Russia	42,330
Messerschmitt Bf 109	Germany	35,000
Vickers Supermarine Spitfire	Britain	20,531
Focke-Wulf Fw 190	Germany	20,000
Consolidated B-24 Liberator	United States	18,000
Yakovlev Yak-9	U.S.S.R.	16,769
Republic P-47 Thunderbolt	United States	15,677
North American P-51 Mustang	United States	15,367
Junkers Ju 88	Germany	15,000
Hawker Hurricane	Britain	14,500
Boeing B-17 Flying Fortress	United States	12,800
Grumman F6F Hellcat	United States	12,275
Mitsubishi Zero	Japan	10,500
Lockheed P-38 Lightning	United States	10,037
Messerschmitt Bf 110	Germany	10,000
North American B-25 Mitchell	United States	9,889
Grumman TBF Avenger	United States	9,836
Grumman F4F Wildcat	United States	7,885
De Havilland Mosquito	Great Britain	7,781
Avro Lancaster	Great Britain	7,377

Substandard Kit

1. CIVIL WAR FOOTWEAR: Some Confederate army issued shoes were made out of wood and stained paper; thousands of soldiers and one lieutenant colonel soon marched barefoot.
2. BRITISH RADIOS: The British army's out-of-date Clansman radio system led one officer to remark in 2001 that the next war "had better be fought in a country with Vodafone coverage."
3. ITALIAN TANK ARMOR: When Italy entered World War II, her tanks and heavy vehicles were so thinly armored that they all could be penetrated by the lightest antitank rifles then in service.
4. GERMAN OVERCOATS: The troops invading the Soviet Union in June 1941 were provided with no winter clothing or antifreeze for their vehicles, as Hitler had assumed the war would be over before the cold set in.
5. ARGENTINE BOMBS: 55 percent of the bombs dropped on the British Task Force during the Falklands War of 1982 failed to explode. Had they detonated, a further six to thirteen ships that were merely damaged might have been sunk and the war lost.

Some Military and Civilian Honors (U.S.)

Medal of Honor
Navy Medal of Honor
Distinguished Service Cross
Navy Cross
Army Distinguished Service Medal
Navy Distinguished Service Medal
Coast Guard Distinguished Service Medal
Silver Star
Legion of Merit
Distinguished Flying Cross
Soldier's Medal
Navy and Marine Corps Medal

Bronze Star
Air Medal
Naval Commendation Medal
Army Commendation Medal
Coast Guard Commendation Medal

The Most Severe Bombing Raids

1. DRESDEN, February 13–14, 1945
   Firebombing by RAF and USAAF, 25,000 dead
2. TOKYO, March 9–10, 1945
   Firebombing by USAAF, 83,000 dead
3. HIROSHIMA, August 6, 1945
   Atomic bomb "Little Boy" dropped by the *Enola Gay,* 78,000 dead
4. HAMBURG, July 24–August 2, 1943
   Firebombing by RAF, 44,000 dead
5. NAGASAKI, August 9, 1945
   Atomic bomb "Fat Man" dropped by *Bock's Car,* 40,000 dead
6. DARMSTADT, September 11, 1944
   Firebombing by RAF and USAAF, 11,000 dead

Total British civilian casualties from air raids over the course of World War II = 60,595

Landmines

Estimated total yet to be defused, per country.

IRAN: 12 million
EGYPT: 7.5 million (after 11 million already cleared)
ANGOLA: 6–9 million
AFGHANISTAN: 4–10 million
VIETNAM: 3.5 million

ZIMBABWE: 2.5 million
ERITREA: 2 million
ETHIOPIA: 2 million
MOROCCO: 2 million
MOZAMBIQUE: 1 million
CAMBODIA: 1 million–6 million
CROATIA: 1 million
BOSNIA-HERZEGOVINA: 1 million
THAILAND: 1 million

There are no official figures for Iraq, but in Iraqi Kurdistan it is estimated that perhaps one person a day steps on a mine.

Notable Warrior Women

1. BOUDICCA: Queen of the Iceni tribe who rebelled against the Roman invasion of Britain in the first century A.D.
2. ZENOBIA: Third-century queen of Palmyra who led her armies to defeat at the hands of Aurelian's Romans. Tried for crimes against the empire, she blamed the counsel of the Greek philosopher Longinus, who was executed in her stead.
3. JOAN OF ARC: Successfully led the French army against the English in the early fifteenth century before her enemies accused her of witchcraft and burned her at the stake when she was nineteen.
4. ISABELLA I OF CASTILE (1451–1504): The Iberian queen wore armor and led her army in the field against rebels early in her reign and later against the Moors alongside her husband, Ferdinand of Aragon.
5. AMELIANE DU PUGET: Governor's daughter who led a troop of women who broke the siege at Marseilles in 1524 during the war between the king of France and the constable de Bourbon. They dug a mined trench known as the Tranchée des Dames that became the Boulevard des Dames.

6. GRAINE NI MAILLE: (Grace O'Malley): Irish princess who commanded a large pirate fleet in the sixteenth century. Queen Elizabeth I of England accepted her territorial claims after the two met in 1593.

7. MARGARET CORBIN: American heroine who fought alongside her husband in the Revolutionary War and was the first woman to receive a pension from the United States government as a disabled soldier.

8. EMILIENNE MOREAU: Fought for the French on the Western Front during World War I. She killed two snipers in the Battle of Loos and was awarded the Croix de Guerre, the British Red Cross Medal, and the St. John Ambulance Society Medal. In 1940 she once again fought for her country, earning a second Croix de Guerre.

9. ELAINE MORDEAUX: Led approximately 200 World War II French Resistance fighters in a guerrilla attack on Germany's 101st Panzer Division. Though few of the French survived, 300 German troops were killed in the assault and about 100 trucks and tanks disabled. The death of Mordeaux and her comrades contributed to the success of the D-day landings as it held up the division's advance to the coast.

10. LUDMILLA PAVLICHENKO: Russian sniper credited with killing 309 Germans during World War II.

11. HANNA REITSCH: The German test pilot was the only woman ever to be awarded the Iron Cross and Luftwaffe Diamond Clasp.

The Crusades

The wars against heretics and infidels between 1095 and 1291 sanctioned by the pope, initially to ensure the safety of Christian pilgrims in the Holy Land.

FIRST CRUSADE, 1095–99: Walter the Penniless and Peter the Hermit fail to reach the Holy Land, but subsequent expeditions establish a Christian kingdom in Asia Minor with Godfrey de Bouillon, Bohemond de Tankerville, and others taking Antioch in 1098 and Jerusalem in 1099.

SECOND CRUSADE, 1147–49: Ended in disaster under Louis VII of France and Conrad III of Germany, who laid siege to Damascus but were driven off with heavy losses after just four days.

THIRD CRUSADE, 1189–92: After Saladin took Damascus in 1174, Aleppo in 1183, and then Jerusalem in 1187, Frederick Barbarossa of Germany invaded through Asia Minor, while Philip Augustus of France and Richard the Lionheart of England landed at Acre and captured the city. After disagreements among the allies, Richard's army was left to fight alone until a truce was concluded.

FOURTH CRUSADE, 1202–4: The crusaders who set out from Venice never reached Jerusalem, but did become embroiled in Venetian politics before sacking Constantinople in 1204 and establishing a Latin empire.

FIFTH CRUSADE, 1217–21: The crusaders invaded Egypt and stormed Damietta in 1219 but then spent a year arguing over the spoils rather than advancing on Cairo. By the time they struck out, their Saracen adversaries had assembled a strong enough force to defeat them and take Damietta for themselves.

SIXTH CRUSADE, 1228–29: Emperor Frederick II had vowed to lead a crusade as early as 1215 but had used a variety of excuses to avoid his commitment. He eventually embarked for the Holy Land in 1227, but returned a few days later citing ill health. Pope Gregory IX excommunicated him for this final impiety, but Frederick honored his vow the following year and in 1229 won Jerusalem, Bethlehem, and Nazareth by entreaty.

SEVENTH CRUSADE, 1249–52: Saint Louis, Louis IX of France, took Damietta but was then himself taken prisoner. He was compelled to relinquish the city and pay a ransom of one million gold bezants.

EIGHTH CRUSADE, 1270: Saint Louis's second mission was hit by the plague soon after he landed at Carthage and was forced to reembark without its fallen leader.

America's Top Ten Defense Contractors (2002)

1. Lockheed Martin Corp.—$17 billion
2. Boeing Co.—$16.6 billion
3. Northrop Grumman Corp.—$8.7 billion
4. Raytheon Co.—$7 billion
5. General Dynamics Corp.—$7 billion
6. United Technologies Corp.—$3.6 billion
7. Science Applications International Corp.—$2.1 billion
8. TRW Inc.—$2 billion
9. Health Net, Inc.—$1.7 billion
10. L-3 Communications Holdings, Inc.—$1.7 billion

Countries Using Child Soldiers

AFGHANISTAN: Preteen combatants fought with Northern Alliance forces.

ANGOLA: Children as young as ten have been forcibly recruited by UNITA rebel and government forces.

BURMA: Orphans under ten are forcibly conscripted.

BURUNDI: Soldiers are sometimes under the official age of eighteen.

COLOMBIA: Up to 15,000 child soldiers fight for the FARC communist rebels.

IVORY COAST: Teens under fifteen fight for rebel groups.

DEMOCRATIC REPUBLIC OF THE CONGO: Rebel forces continue to recruit children.

GUINEA-BISSAU: Boys under sixteen can volunteer for military service with the consent of their parents or tutors.

IRAQ: Before the 2003 Iraq War, boys who did not volunteer for weapons training in the Saddam Cubs were denied ration cards and exam results.

LIBERIA: Armed militias forcibly recruit children.

NEPAL: Teenagers are recruited by Maoist rebels.

PARAGUAY: Up to 100 conscripts under eighteen have died since 1989.

PHILIPPINES: Rebel and Islamic groups commandeer fighters as young as eleven.

SUDAN: Government and rebel forces conscript teenagers.

UGANDA: Government can enlist boys under eighteen with parental consent. The rebel Lord's Resistance Army is notorious for abducting preteens and using them as guerrillas and sex slaves.

Epitaphs

The Confederate epitaph:

Not for fame or reward, not for place or rank, not lured by ambition or goaded by necessity, but in simple obedience to duty as they understood it, these men suffered all, sacrificed all . . . and died. (Arlington National Cemetery)

The Kohima epitaph:

> When you go home, tell them of us and say,
> For their tomorrow, we gave our today.

Written by John Maxwell Edmonds in 1919, inscribed on the Second World War memorial in Kohima, India.

To the 300 Spartans:

> Go tell the Spartans, you who pass by,
> that here, obedient to their laws, we lie.

Written by Simonides of Kios, inscribed at the Pass of Thermopylae, which they held in 480 B.C.

The Winds of War

1. THE LOST ARMY OF CAMBYSES: In 523 B.C., the Persian emperor Cambyses sent 50,000 men across Egypt's western desert to destroy the oracle of Amun at Siwa. The army vanished, presumably swallowed by a great sandstorm.
2. THE WINDS OF CARTHAGE: In 262 B.C. the Roman invasion fleet of Marcus Atilius Regulus was destroyed by a storm on its way to Africa with the loss of 100,000 lives.
3. THE DIVINE WIND (*kamikaze*): Typhoons destroyed the Mongol invasion fleets that attacked Japan in 1274 and 1281. The first comprised 900 ships and 40,000 troops; the second was made up of 4,000 vessels and 140,000 troops.
4. THE ENGLISH WINDS: The storm that scattered the Spanish Armada fleet in 1588 caused Philip II to lament that "God is an Englishman."

The Kamikaze's Prebattle Ritual

1. Don white headscarf with rising sun motif.
2. Wind around waist the belt of a thousand stitches, crafted by a thousand women making one stitch each.
3. Drink a cup of sake.
4. Compose and recite death poem—traditional for samurai prior to hara-kiri.

Suicidal Pseudonyms

Names for Japan's World War II kamikaze rocket planes.

Ohka (cherry blossom)
Jinrai (thunderbolt)
Baka (idiot; given by the Allies to refer to the suicidal pilot)

Around 5,000 kamikaze pilots are thought to have died during World War II.

"The Young British Soldier" by Rudyard Kipling

> When you're wounded and left on Afghanistan's plains,
> And the women come out to cut up what remains,
> Jest roll to your rifle and blow out your brains
>   An' go to your Gawd like a soldier.

The Lost Regiments

Confederate units that bore the heaviest casualties in the American Civil War.

1st Texas	Sharpsburg	82.3%
21st Georgia	Manassas	76
26th North Carolina	Gettysburg	71.7
6th Mississippi	Shiloh	70.5
8th Tennessee	Stones River	68.2
10th Tennessee	Chickamauga	68
Palmetto Sharpshooters	Glendale	67.7
17th South Carolina	Manassas	66.9
23rd South Carolina	Manassas	66.2
44th Georgia	Mechanicsville	65.1

Military Ranks

Army

General of the Army
General
Lieutenant General
Major General
Brigadier General
Colonel
Lieutenant Colonel
Major
Captain
First Lieutenant
Second Lieutenant
Chief Warrant Officer CW-5
Chief Warrant Officer CW-4
Chief Warrant Officer CW-2
Warrant Officer WO-1

Sergeant Major of the Army
Command Sergeant Major and Sergeant Major
First Sergeant, Master Sergeant
Sergeant First Class
Staff Sergeant
Sergeant
Corporal, Specialist
Private First Class
Private

Marines

Commandant of the Marine Corps
General
Lieutenant General
Major General
Brigadier General
Colonel
Lieutenant Colonel
Major
Captain
First Lieutenant
Second Lieutenant
Chief Warrant Officer
Sergeant Major of the Marine Corps
Sergeant Major
Master Gunnery Sergeant
First Sergeant
Master Sergeant
Gunnery Sergeant
Staff Sergeant
Sergeant
Corporal
Lance Corporal
Private First Class
Private

Navy

Fleet Admiral
Admiral
Vice Admiral
Rear Admiral Upper Half
Rear Admiral Lower Half
Captain
Commander
Lieutenant Commander
Lieutenant
Lieutenant Junior Grade
Ensign
Midshipman
Chief Warrant Officer 4
Chief Warrant Officer 3
Chief Warrant Officer 2
Master Chief Petty Officer of the Navy, Master Chief Petty
    Officer
Senior Chief Petty Officer
Chief Petty Officer
Petty Officer First Class
Petty Officer Second Class
Petty Officer Third Class
Seaman, Airman, Fireman, Constructionman
Seaman Apprentice, Airman Apprentice, Fireman Apprentice,
    Constructionman Apprentice
Seaman Recruit, Airman Recruit, Fireman Recruit,
    Constructionman Recruit

Air Force

General of the Air Force
General
Lieutenant General
Major General

Brigadier General
Colonel
Lieutenant Colonel
Major
Captain
First Lieutenant
Second Lieutenant
Chief Master Sergeant of the Air Force, Command Chief
Master Sergeant, Chief Master Sergeant
Senior Master Sergeant
Master Sergeant
Technical Sergeant
Staff Sergeant
Senior Airman
Airman First Class
Airman
Airman Basic

Alliances

NATO: North Atlantic Treaty Organization (formed in 1949; membership as of 2003)

Belgium	Italy
Canada	Luxembourg
Czech Republic	Netherlands
Denmark	Norway
France (withdrew from the	Poland
military structure in 1966)	Portugal
Germany	Spain
Greece	Turkey
Hungary	United Kingdom
Iceland	United States

SEATO: South East Asia Treaty Organization (1954–77)

Australia
France
Great Britain
New Zealand
Pakistan
Philippines
Thailand
United States

The Warsaw Pact (1955–91)

Albania (left in 1961)
Bulgaria
Czechoslovakia
East Germany
Hungary
Poland
Romania
U.S.S.R.

The Arab League (1945–)

Algeria
Bahrain
Comoros
Djibouti
Egypt*
Iraq*
Jordan*
Kuwait
Lebanon*
Libya (withdrew 2002)
Mauritania
Morocco
Oman
Palestine (PLO)
Qatar
Saudi Arabia*
Somalia
Sudan
Syria*
Tunisia
United Arab Emirates
Yemen*

*founder members

ECOWAS: Economic Community of West African States (1975–)

Benin	Liberia
Burkina Faso	Mali
Cape Verde	Niger
Gambia	Nigeria
Ghana	Senegal
Guinea	Sierra Leone
Guinea-Bissau	Togolese Republic
Ivory Coast	

The Anzus Pact (1951–84)

Australia
New Zealand
United States

Phrases of Warfare

Go the full nine yards: When a World War II fighter pilot fired off all his ammunition—9 yards of it—in one burst.

Dressed up to the nines: After the eighteenth-century British 99th Foot regiment, whose officers were said to be particularly well dressed.

Freeze the balls off a brass monkey: Cannonballs were once kept in a brass rack (or monkey), which contracted when cold, ejecting the balls.

Pyrrhic victory: Named after the ancient Greek king Pyrrhus of Epirus, who won a series of victories against the Romans that gradually depleted his veteran troops until they could no longer be replaced and he was finally defeated at Beneventum in 275 B.C.

Hip, hip, hooray!: Alleged to have been shouted by the Crusaders to mean "Jerusalem is lost to the infidel, and we are on our

way to paradise"—HIP or HEP being an acronym for
Hierosolyma est perdita.

Gung ho: From the Chinese for "working together."

Hooker: From "Fighting" Joe Hooker, the Union general who
showed such zeal in rounding up Washington's ladies of the
night.

Casus belli: Cause of war.

Learning the ropes: New sailors getting used to the rigging on
sailing ships.

Scuttlebutt: The cask of drinking water onboard ship, around
which sailors would gather and gossip.

Show one's true colors: From men-of-war that would approach an
enemy ship while flying a friendly flag, then hoist their true
flag immediately prior to opening fire.

Son of a gun: In the days when women were allowed to live
aboard naval vessels, children born at sea of unknown fathers
were entered into the ship's log as "son of a gun."

Filibuster: The name given to an individual waging war without
government sanction in mid-nineteenth-century Latin
America.

Freelance: A medieval knight without a lord or lands of his own.

Minutemen: Colonial militia during the American Revolutionary
War, so called for their instant readiness.

Quisling: From Vidkun Quisling, founder of the Norwegian
Fascist National Union Party and collaborationist leader of
his country under German occupation after February 1942.

Turncoat: A duke of Saxony whose lands bordered France
supposedly once dressed his men in blue coats that had a
white interior, one to which they could switch when he wanted
them to be thought to be acting in the French interest.

Under the yoke: The Romans would force the troops of a
defeated army to pass under a yoke (archway) of three spears
to demonstrate their submission.

Vandal: From the Teutonic tribe that sacked Rome for two
weeks in 455.

Gazetted: To have news of one's award for bravery published in the London *Gazette.*

Uncle Sam: During the War of 1812 a New York butcher named Samuel Wilson shipped pork to the army in kegs stamped "U.S." Wilson was known as Uncle Sam, though the white-haired figure familiar from recruitment posters was modeled after Dan Rice, a professional clown with the Barnum and Bailey circus.

V for Victory: The two-fingered victory salute originates from the gesture used by English archers to taunt the French at Agincourt in 1415; captured yeomen would have their index and middle fingers amputated so that they could never draw a bowstring again.

U.S. Presidents of Military Rank (*in order of presidency*)

George Washington, Lieutenant General*
James Madison, Colonel
James Monroe, Lieutenant Colonel
Andrew Jackson, Major General
William H. Harrison, Major General
John Tyler, Captain (militia)
Zachary Taylor, Major General
Franklin Pierce, Brigadier General
James Buchanan, Private
Abraham Lincoln, Captain (militia)
Andrew Johnson, Brigadier General†
Ulysses S. Grant, General of the Army
Rutherford B. Hayes, Major General
James A. Garfield, Major General
Chester A. Arthur, Quartermaster General
Benjamin Harrison, Brigadier General
William McKinley, Major
Theodore Roosevelt, Colonel

Harry S. Truman, Major
Dwight D. Eisenhower, General of the Army
John F. Kennedy, Lieutenant (Navy)
Lyndon B. Johnson, Lieutenant Commander (Navy)
Richard M. Nixon, Lieutenant Commander (Navy)
Gerald R. Ford, Lieutenant Commander (Navy)
Jimmy Carter, Lieutenant (Navy)
Ronald W. Reagan, Captain
George Bush, Lieutenant (Navy)
George W. Bush, Lieutenant (National Guard)

*posthumously promoted six-star General of the Armies by Congress in 1976
† As military governor of Tennessee

Military Acronyms and Abbreviations

ABM—Anti-Ballistic Missile
AEF—American Expeditionary Force
AMRAAM—Advanced Medium Range Air-to-Air Missile
ANZAC—Australia and New Zealand Army Corps
ASDIC—Anti-Submarine Detection and Identification Commission
AWACS—Airborne Warning and Control System
AWOL—Absent Without Official Leave
BEF—British Expeditionary Force
CIA—Central Intelligence Agency
CIGS—Chief of the Imperial General Staff
CINCUS—Commander in Chief, U.S. Fleet (abolished in 1941
     when its proximity to "sink us" was noticed)
CTBT—Comprehensive Test Ban Treaty
DEFCON—Defense Condition
DMZ—Demilitarized zone
GCHQ—Government Communications Headquarters
GI—There are three derivations from the legends stamped on
     several pieces of the U.S. Army issue kit during World War II:
     Government Issue, General Issue, Galvanized Iron.

HALO—High Altitude Low Opening parachute jump

ICBM—Intercontinental Ballistic Missile

KGB—Committee for State Security (U.S.S.R.) (formerly NKVD)

KIA—Killed in Action

LAW—Light Antitank Weapon

MASH—Mobile Army Surgical Hospital

Medevac—Medical evacuation

MIA—Missing in Action

MOAB—Massive Ordnance Aerial Bomb (Mother Of All
    Bombs, colloquially)

MRE—Meals Ready-to-Eat

NAAFI—Navy, Army and Air Force Institute

NKVD—People's Commissariat of Internal Affairs (U.S.S.R.)
    (became the KGB in 1953)

NORAD—North American Air Defense Command

OSS—Office of Strategic Services

PIAT—Projectile Infantry Anti-Tank weapon

RADAR—Radio Detecting and Ranging

SA—Sturm Abteilung (Storm Detachment)

SALT—Strategic Arms Limitations Talks

SAS—Special Air Service

SBS—Special Boat Service

SHAEF—Supreme Headquarters Allied Expeditionary Force

SLBM—Submarine-Launched Ballistic Missile

SMERSH—A contraction of Smyert Shpionam ("Death to Spies"),
    Soviet counterintelligence organization disbanded in 1958

SOE—Special Operations Executive

SONAR—Sound, Navigation and Ranging

SOS—Save Our Souls (the letters were originally meaningless,
    chosen because they were easy to remember in Morse code).

SS—Schutzstaffel (Protection Squad)

SSM—Surface-to-Surface Missile

START—Strategic Arms Reduction Talks

UNPROFOR—United Nations Protection Force

UNSCOM—United Nations Special Commission

Military Mascots and Pets

1. BOY: A white dog that accompanied Prince Rupert into battle during the English Civil War and brought good luck to the Cavaliers. The Roundheads regarded him as an evil spirit and celebrated when he was killed in action at Marston Moor in 1644.

2. SATAN: A greyhound that saved a vital French position at Verdun in 1916 by bringing carrier pigeons to help direct defensive artillery fire despite having been shot by an enemy sniper.

3. PRINCE: An Irish terrier that went missing from his London home in 1914 and tracked down his master, Private James Brown of the North Staffordshire Regiment, in Armentières, France, a few weeks later.

4. BLONDI: The Alsatian dog beloved of Adolf Hitler whom the Führer like to teach tricks.

5. ZUCHA: A Stakhanovite Russian dog that "inspired other hounds" by finding 2,000 mines in eighteen days during World War II.

6. VOYTEK: A Syrian bear and mascot of the 2nd Polish Transport Company that trapped an enemy spy attempting to raid the company's ammunition supply in Iraq in 1942.

7. BUCEPHALUS: The steed of Alexander the Great. Alexander was the only man who could tame the horse, which he did after noticing that it was afraid of its own shadow and turned its head toward the sun. When, at thirty years of age, Bucephalus died of wounds after carrying his master to safety, he was buried with full military honors.

8. INCITATUS: The Roman emperor Caligula's horse, which the tyrant made a consul. Incitatus had an ivory manger and drank wine from a golden goblet.

9. THE HARTLEPOOL MONKEY: In 1805, the French ship the *Chasse Marée* was wrecked in a storm off the English coastal town of Hartlepool. When the vessel's mascot—a small monkey dressed in a miniature uniform—was washed up on shore, local fishermen

believed it to be a French spy and, and after holding an im-
promptu trial, summarily executed the creature by hanging.

10. LASSIE: In 1915 the bodies of 500 British seamen killed in
action were stacked in Lyme Regis, England, to await burial.
A sheepdog named Lassie—the inspiration for Eric Knight's
fictional hound—began to lick the face of one of the sailors,
who proved to be still alive and survived after being rushed
to the hospital.

World Wars

**Conflicts in which all the great powers of the time
were involved.**

1. The Thirty Years' War, 1618–48
2. The War of the Spanish Succession, 1701–14
3. The Seven Years' War, 1756–63
4. The Revolutionary and Napoleonic wars, 1791–1815
5. The First World War, 1914–18
6. The Second World War, 1939–45

Praised by GIs Billeted in England During the Second World War

Fish and chips
The 4 o'clock tea break
The London Underground
British hospitality
Pubs

Common Complaints of GIs Billeted in England During the Second World War

Watery coffee
Warm beer
Tasteless meat pies
Disgusting Brussels sprouts
Greasy mutton
Blackout conditions
The locals' shabby clothing
Impenetrable fog
Shiny, non-absorbent toilet tissue
Lunchtime closing for shops
The bad teeth and body odor of English girls (though some
    70,000 were taken home as brides)
Being expected to fraternize with black servicemen

Yanks Bearing Gifts

The most popular luxuries supplied by GIs to the English during World War II.

Silk stockings
Chewing gum
Tinned fruit
Coca-Cola
Absorbent toilet tissue
Candy and chocolate
Cigarettes

How to Lose the Second World War:
The Crucial Mistakes of Adolf Hitler

1. INVADING POLAND: He believed the Western powers would re-nege on their promises to intervene on his victim's behalf.

2. DUNKIRK: Hitler allowed the British army and thousands of French troops to escape across the English Channel between May 26 and June 3, 1940.

3. OPERATION SEA LION: Failure to press ahead with the plan to invade Great Britain, which would have denied the United States her largest, unsinkable aircraft carrier and springboard for the liberation of Western Europe.

4. OPERATION BARBAROSSA: Invading the Soviet Union in June 1941 and facing the Russian winter unprepared.

5. STALINGRAD: The order that von Paulus's army should fight and die to the last man in the ruined city.

6. NORTH AFRICA: The failure to support Rommel, and the sub-sequent refusal to allow him to withdraw, cost him the North African armies and access to Middle Eastern oil.

7. THE SLEEPING GIANT: Declaring war on the United States on September 11, 1941.

8. D-DAY: Declined to bring the full weight of the Wermacht to bear on the Allied beachhead, believing it to be a diversion.

9. RACISM: His views on Aryan racial supremacy led him to spurn the talents of Germany's Jewish population and the Slavs who initially welcomed the German invaders of the Soviet Union as liberators.

The Civil War Goes On

The chief military actions that took place after General Robert E. Lee surrendered on April 9, 1865.

APRIL 10: At Mobile, Alabama, Federal forces under Edward Canby bombard Fort Huger and Fort Tracy. The 5,000 Confederate defenders surrender on April 12.

APRIL 12: James Wilson's cavalry occupy Montgomery, Alabama Stoneman's Union army attacks Grant's Creek.

APRIL 13: In Mobile, a Confederate torpedo sinks the Union ship *Ida*.

APRIL 15: Wilson captures Columbus, Georgia.

APRIL 17: Federal navy destroys the Confederate ironclads CSS *Muscogee* and *Jackson*.

APRIL 20: Wilson occupies Macon, Georgia. Skirmish at Rocky Creek Bridge, Alabama.

APRIL 21: Gray Ghost John Singleton Mosby refuses to surrender and instead disbands his Rangers at Millwood, Virginia, to preserve their honor.

APRIL 22: Wilson's cavalry occupies Talladega, Alabama.

APRIL 26: Joe Johnston's 30,000-strong Confederate army surrenders to Sherman. The *Sultana*, carrying hundreds of paroled Federal soldiers home, exploded with the loss of 1,900 lives, allegedly due to Confederate sabotage.

MAY 4: General Richard Taylor surrenders his Confederate Mississippi-Louisiana-Alabama force and General Forrest's cavalry to General Canby. Skirmishes near Lexington, Missouri, and at Wetumpka, Alabama.

MAY 10: President Davis is captured near Irwinville, Georgia. CSA General Samuel Jones surrenders his command at Tallahassee, Florida. Confederate guerrilla leader William Clarke Quantrill is fatally wounded near Taylorsville, Kentucky.

MAY 11: General Jeff Thompson surrenders his brigade.

MAY 12: Colonel John Ford's Confederates defeat Colonel Theodore Barrett's Federal troops in the Battle of Palmito Ranch, on the banks of the Rio Grande in Texas.

MAY 20: Federal troops battle Confederate guerrillas in Blackwater, Missouri.

JUNE 2: LSA General Edmund Kirby Smith officially accepts the surrender terms onboard Union steamer *Fort Jackson* at Galveston harbor, and hands over his sword to the Union commander General Edward Canby.

JUNE 3: The Confederate navy in Red River officially surrenders.

JUNE 23: The last significant Confederate land force—the Cherokee leader General Stand Watie's Native Americans— surrenders at Doaksville near Fort Towson in Indian Territory (Oklahoma).

JUNE 22: The last shot of the war is fired by the CSS *Shenandoah*, whose commander, Captain James Waddell, finally learned of the Confederacy's defeat on August 2. He refused to surrender his vessel and sailed westward around the world until he reached the safety of Liverpool, England, on November 5.

JULY: General Jo Shelby leads several hundred Confederates to the Rio Grande and Mexico.

American Soil Attacked or Occupied by the Axis Powers during the Second World War

1. KISKA AND ATTU: Two of the Aleutian Islands off Alaska were occupied by the Japanese in June 1942.

2. BROOKINGS, OREGON: In September 1942, a Japanese seaplane piloted by Nobuo Fujita dropped incendiary bombs that started a forest fire. Fujita returned to the area after the war, where the locals praised him as an "ambassador of goodwill" and made him an honorary citizen. He later organized student exchanges.

3. CALIFORNIA: Signal Hill and Goleta were subjected to Japanese naval bombardments.

4. THE ROCKY MOUNTAINS: Japan sent balloon bombs that traveled as far as the Rockies. One such device killed a picnicking family.

5. COLORADO: In 1942 it was discovered that Adolf Hitler owned 9,000 acres of grazing land that he had inherited from relatives.

A Short History of Chemical Warfare

The use of chemical warfare in World War I was pioneered by Fritz Haber, a Prussian Jew who went on to win the Nobel Prize for Chemistry in 1919 "for the synthesis of ammonia from its elements." On April 22, 1915, Haber was at the front lines directing the first gas attack in military history. About 150 tons of chlorine blew across the fields of Flanders, Belgium, spreading panic and death among the British and French soldiers. Haber returned to Berlin with his new technology apparently vindicated. A few days later, on May 15, his wife, Clara, appalled by his "perversion of science," shot herself. Haber later invented Zyklon-B, the gas used by the Nazis to effect the Holocaust.

Some of the instances of chemical warfare:

1. TEAR GAS: In August 1914, the first month of World War I, the Germans claimed that the French fired tear gas grenades at their positions. In fact the French police (not army) had used tear gas before the war.

2. "SNEEZING POWDER": In the capture of Neuve Chapelle in October 1914 the German army fired shells at the French containing a chemical irritant that induced violent sneezing fits.

3. CHLORINE GAS: The first use of chlorine gas was on April 22, 1915, at the start of the Second Battle of Ypres. Used by the Germans against French and Algerian troops, the gas created a four-mile gap in the Allied lines.

4. PHOSGENE: First used in December 1915 by Germany. Its effects could be delayed for up to two days. Soldiers often inhaled lethal doses without realizing they had been gassed.

5. MUSTARD GAS: First used by Germany against the Russians at Riga in September 1917. Unlike its predecessors, mustard gas did not have to be inhaled. An almost odorless chemical, it caused serious blisters both in the lungs and on any moist skin. Mussolini's victory in Abyssinia in 1937 was aided by the use of mustard gas bombs dropped from aircraft.

6. TABUN: The first nerve agent was discovered by German chemist Gerhard Schrader in 1936. He almost died after his assistant spilled a single drop of Tabun.

7. VX NERVE GAS: After its discovery by the British in 1952, the manufacture of VX began in quantity in the United States in 1961. Production ceased in 1968, when an accident at the plant in Dugway, Utah, caused a cloud of the agent to be blown toward a nearby town, killing 6,000 sheep.

8. AGENT ORANGE: Used along with Agent Purple, Agent Blue, and Agent White by U.S. forces during the Vietnam War from 1965–75 to defoliate the vegetation surrounding the enemy.

9. CHEMICAL AND NERVE GAS: In 1988, Iraqi jet fighters dropped chemical and nerve gas on Halabja after the village fell into the hands of Kurdish rebels. More than 5,000 people died.

10. SARIN: In 1995, Japan's Aum Shinrikyo religious cult released sarin nerve gas in Tokyo's subway system during morning rush hour. Eleven people died and more than 5,500 were injured.

One-Sided Victories

1. THE BATTLE OF MARATHON, 490 B.C.: When 10,000 Athenians defeated the 25,000 Persians of Darius the Great on the Plain of Marathon, they lost only 192 men to the enemy's 6,400.

2. THE TEARLESS BATTLE, 368 B.C.: Spartan king Archidamnus III routed a combined force of Argives and Arcadians without a single loss among his troops.

3. CANNAE, 216 B.C.: 80,000 Romans under consuls Varro and Paulus were encircled by Hannibal's Carthaginian army. Upwards of 70,000 were killed in the republic's heaviest defeat. Hannibal lost only 5,700 men.

4. THE BATTLE OF MAGNESIA, 190 B.C.: Lucius Cornelius Scipio invaded Asia Minor with 30,000 troops to be met by a Seleucid force under Antiochus, numbering 72,000 (supported by scythed chariots and 54 elephants), of which 53,000 were killed with a loss of only 350 Romans.

5. ICENI REVOLT: According to Tacitus, in A.D. 61 a Roman army of 10,000 put down Queen Boudicca's rebellion, losing 400 men while slaughtering 80,000 Britons.

6. THE BATTLE OF ARGENTORATUM, 357: 13,000 Romans under Julian defeated 35,000 German Alamanni tribesmen, killing 6,000 Alamanni with a loss of only 247 Romans.

7. THE BATTLE OF JACINTO, 1836: General Sam Houston attacked with 783 men and defeated 1,500 Mexicans who had been ordered to take a siesta by General Antonio López de Santa Anna. Although the battle lasted only eighteen minutes, 630 men of the Mexican army were killed; the Texans lost only 9.

8. THE SHORTEST WAR EVER: In 1896 a usurper seized the throne of Zanzibar for precisely 45 minutes. A naval bombardment from three British warships destroyed the sultan's palace and the usurper fled.

9. THE BATTLE OF OMDURMAN, 1898: An Anglo-Egyptian force of 26,000 men armed with machine guns and artillery met an army of 40,000 Mahdist Sudanese armed with swords and lances. The latter suffered 10,000 killed, 10,000 wounded, and 5,000 taken prisoner, while the British had only 500 casualties.

10. THE PERSIAN GULF WAR, 1991: U.S. and coalition forces lost 239 dead while inflicting more than 100,000 casualties on the Iraqi army during the liberation of Kuwait.

Ten of the Bloodiest Wars

1. THE SECOND WORLD WAR, 1939–45: c. 45 million deaths (including deaths in the Holocaust)

2. THE T'AI P'ING REBELLION, 1851–64: c. 30 million deaths. The bloodiest ever civil war claimed between 20 million and 40 million Chinese lives. Hung Hsiu-Ch'uan, the defeated rebel leader, believed himself to be Jesus Christ's younger brother.

3. THE MANCHU CHINESE WAR, 1644–90s: c. 25 million. Marked the end of the Ming dynasty.

4. THE FIRST WORLD WAR 1914–18: c. 15 million deaths.

5. THE NAPOLEONIC WARS, 1792–1815: c. 5 million (including the French Revolution).

6. THE THIRTY YEARS' WAR, 1618–48: c. 4 million

7. THE LOPEZ WAR, 1864–70: c. 2 million. During the war between Paraguay and the Triple Alliance of Argentina, Brazil, and Peru, Paraguay's population was reduced from 1,337,000 to 221,000.

8. THE SUDANESE CIVIL WAR, 1983–   : c. 1.9 million deaths. One in five southern Sudanese have died as a result of the conflict and the associated famine.

9. THE CONGOLESE CIVIL WAR, 1998–   : c. 1.7 million deaths. Between 1998 and 2003, an estimated 200,000 were killed in the fighting, with a further 1.5 million succumbing to disease and starvation as a result of hostilities.

10. THE SEVEN YEARS' WAR, 1756–63: c. 1.4 million deaths. Between 1756 and 1962, the population of Prussia declined by half a million.

Mottoes

U.S. MARINE CORPS: Semper fidelis (Always faithful)

U.S. ARMY CORPS OF ENGINEERS: Essayons (Let us try)

RAF: Per ardua ad astra (Through difficulties to the stars)

617 SQUADRON (DAMBUSTERS) RAF: Après moi, le déluge (After me, the flood)

PARACHUTE REGIMENT: Utrimque paratus (the "Red Devils") (Ready for anything)

ROYAL ARMY MEDICAL CORPS: In arduis fidelis (Faithful in adversity)

SPECIAL AIR SERVICE (SAS): Who dares wins

U.S. ARMY SPECIAL FORCES: De oppresso liber (To free the oppressed)

SEVERAL SCOTTISH REGIMENTS: Nemo me impune lacessit (Nobody insults me [and the Scottish Crown] with impunity)

KING'S REGIMENT: Nec aspera terrent (Difficulties be damned)

ROYAL IRISH REGIMENT: Faugh-a-ballagh (Clear the way)

KING'S OWN SCOTTISH: Once a Borderer, always a Borderer

COLDSTREAM GUARDS: Second to None

U.S. AIR FORCE SECURITY FORCE: Defensor fortis (Defender of the force)

ROYAL MARINES: Per Mare, Per Terram (By Sea, By Land)

ROYAL NAVY SUBMARINE SERVICE: We Come Unseen

ROYAL GURKHA RIFLES: Better to Die than Be a Coward

U.S. NAVY ADMIRAL WILLIAM F. HALSEY, JR.: Hit hard, hit fast, hit often

WEST POINT MILITARY ACADEMY: Duty, honor, country

HITLER'S SS: Meine Ehre heißt Treue (My honor is loyalty)

Countries with Mandatory National Service
(with no nonmilitary alternative)

Afghanistan
Albania
Algeria
Bolivia
Cambodia
Chile
China
Colombia
Cuba
Dominican
    Republic
Ecuador
Egypt
Equatorial
    Guinea
Ethiopia
Georgia

Greece
Guatemala
Guinea
Guinea-Bissau
Honduras
Iran
Iraq
Israel*
Kazakhstan
South Korea
Laos
Lebanon
Liberia
Libya
Madagascar
Mexico
Mongolia

Morocco
Mozambique
North Korea
Paraguay
Peru
Philippines
Romania
Singapore
Somalia
Sudan
Thailand
Tunisia
Turkey
Venezuela
Vietnam
Yemen

*In Israel, strictly orthodox Jews can find exemption from military service.

The Casualties and Costs of the First World War

Nation	Troops mobilized	Military dead	Military wounded	Civilian dead
France	8,410,000	1,357,000	4,266,000	40,000
British Empire	8,904,467	908,000	2,090,212	30,633
Russia	12,000,000	1,700,000	4,950,000	2,000,000
Italy	5,615,000	462,391	953,886	Unknown
United States	4,355,000	50,585	205,690	–
Belgium	267,000	13,715	44,686	30,000
Serbia	707,343	45,000	133,148	650,000
Montenegro	50,000	3,000	10,000	Unknown
Romania	750,000	335,706	120,000	275,000
Greece	230,000	5,000	21,000	132,000
Portugal	100,000	7,222	13,751	–
Japan	800,000	300 907	–	
Allied Total	42,188,810	4,887,919	12,809,280	3,157,633
Germany	11,000,000	1,808,546	4,247,143	760,000
Austria-Hungary	7,800,000	922,500	3,620,000	300,000
Turkey	2,850,000	325,000	400,000	2,150,000
Bulgaria	1,200,000	75,844	152,390	275,000
Central Powers Total	22,850,000	3,131,889	8,419,533	3,485,000
Grand Total	65,038,810	8,020,780	21,228,813	6,642,633

The Casualties and Costs of the Second World War

Nation	Troops mobilized (millions)	Military dead	Military wounded	Civilian dead
United States	14.9	292,100	571,822	–
United Kingdom	6.2	397,762	475,000	65,000
France	6	210,671	400,000	108,000
U.S.S.R.	25	7,500,000	14,012,000	10–15,000,000
China	6–10	500,000	1,700,000	1,000,000
Germany	12.5	2,850,000	7,250,000	500,000
Italy	4.5	77,000	120,000	40–100,000
Japan	7.4	1,506,000	500,000	300,000
Others	20	1,500,000	–	14–17,000,000*
Total	105	15,000,000	25,028,822	26–34,000,000

*Includes 6 million European Jews and 4.5 million Poles.

Impossible Odds

1. THE SPARTANS OF THERMOPYLAE, 480 B.C.: 300 warriors under Leonidas defended the pass of Thermopylae for two days against several hundred thousand soldiers from Xerxes I's Persian army. They inflicted a reported 20,000 casualties and gave their countrymen enough time to prepare their navies to fight and win the Battle of Salamis.
2. THE BATTLE OF JINGXING PASS, 204 B.C.: The fortified pass was held by the Zhao general Chen Yu with 200,000 soldiers. Han Xin routed them using only 12,000 of his troops, who succeeded in convincing the enemy that they were facing a much larger force.
3. THE BATTLE OF SHAYUAN, A.D. 537: The western Chinese Wei warlord Yuwen Tai led an army of 10,000 against the 200,000 men of his eastern rival Gao Huan, defeating them by killing 6,000.

4. THE BATTLE OF GUADALETE, 711: 12,300 Berbers and Arabs under Tarik ibn Ziyad defeated Visigoth King Roderic's army of 90,000. The Jews of Toledo welcomed the Muslim conquerors as liberators.

5. THE NORMAN CONQUEST OF ENGLAND, 1066–70: William assembled an army of around 7,000 to 8,000 Normans, making a total of 10,000 including later arrivals, who went on to subdue a country of approximately 1.5 million people.

6. THE SIEGE OF DE-AN, 1206–7: The southern Chinese city was successfully defended by 6,000 troops under Wang Yunchu against 100,000 northern Jurchen attackers who employed siege towers and trebuchets.

7. THE MONGOLS: By 1215, Genghis Khan had conquered the Jin empire in China with 75,000 soldiers against 600,000.

8. THE BATTLE OF AUBEROCHE, 1345: During the Hundred Years' War, the Earl of Derby with 1,200 troops routed a French army of 7,000 that was besieging Auberoche in southwestern France, capturing the enemy commander Louis of Poitiers.

9. THE BATTLE OF KAUTHAL, 1367: 40,000 Muslim troops mustered by the Bahmani sultanate bested 540,000 Hindus from the kingdom of Vijayanagar by superior cavalry action when most of their fellows had already been routed.

10. THE BATTLE OF AGINCOURT, 1415: 900 men at arms and 5,000 archers commanded by Henry V of England defeated 20,000 French troops.

11. THE CONQUEST OF MEXICO: In 1521, Hernán Cortés landed with 550 Spaniards and went on to conquer an Aztec empire of 11 million subjects.

12. THE CONQUEST OF PERU: In 1532, Francisco Pizarro landed with 150 Spaniards and captured the Inca capital Cajamarca, killing 7,000 enemy troops with no losses among his own men.

13. THE BATTLE OF ASSAYE, 1803: The Duke of Wellington, with 7,000 men and 20 cannon, prevailed against 75,000 Indian Marathas with 80 cannon.

14. THE ALAMO, 1836: Over a thirteen-day siege, 189 men—including Jim Bowie and Davy Crockett—fought to the death against over 2,000 Mexican troops under Santa Anna. In the process they inflicted more than 1,000 casualties and bought time for the defense of Texas.

15. THE SABINE PASS, TEXAS, 1863: 43 Confederate soldiers with 6 cannon under Captain Richard W. Dowling drove off a Federal force of 15,000 men attempting to land, without losing a single man of their own.

16. RORKE'S DRIFT, 1879: 150 British redcoats successfully defended a supply station against 4,000 Zulus. Eleven Victoria Crosses were awarded for the action.

17. GERONIMO: The Apache guerrilla leader, with only 35 braves and some 100 women and children in tow, eluded and held off General Nelson Miles's 5,000 U.S. and 500 Native American troops for five months in Arizona and New Mexico before his surrender in 1886.

18. EAST AFRICA, 1914–18: German General Paul von Lettow-Vorbeck's force of 3,000 European troops and 11,000 Africans remained undefeated by Allied armies totaling more than 300,000 men over the course of World War I. Though their rifle strength was only 1,400 at the time of the armistice, they inflicted 60,000 British and Indian casualties and an unrecorded number of African casualties.

Rome's Civil Wars

1. THE ITALIAN SOCIAL WAR, 91–88 B.C.: Rome's allies who were refused citizenship rebelled and were defeated.

2. SULLA'S REVOLT, 88–82 B.C.: Sulla turned his legions on Rome after a dispute with Marius and won victory after the latter's death.

3. CAESAR AND POMPEY, 49–45 B.C.: When Julius Caesar declined to be prosecuted for his behavior as consul of Gaul and

instead led his forces against the empire, Pompey the Great joined the battle against him. Pompey's armies fought on for three years after their master was murdered.

4. ANTONY AND OCTAVIAN, 44–31 B.C.: The armies of Mark Antony and Octavian defeated Brutus and Cassius, the coconspirators in the murder of Julius Caesar. The two leaders then fell out, in part due to Antony's relationship with the Egyptian queen Cleopatra. Octavian became the undisputed ruler of Rome after the Battle of Actium.

The Punic Wars, Rome versus Carthage

FIRST PUNIC WAR, 264–241 B.C.: After a series of sea battles, Rome gains control of Sicily.

SECOND PUNIC WAR, 218–201 B.C.: Hannibal defeats Rome at Trebia, Lake Trasimene, and Cannae before losing to Scipio Africanus at Zama in 202 B.C.

THIRD PUNIC WAR, 149–146 B.C.: After a three-year siege, the population of Carthage was sold into slavery and the city razed to the ground.

Arms and Armor of a Roman Legionary

BALTEUS: military belt

CALIGAE: hobnailed leather sandals

CASSIS: helmet

FOCALE: scarf worn to protect the neck against chafing from armor

GLADIUS: short sword

LORICA: body armor for the torso

MANICA: segmented arm guard

OCREAE: shin-protecting greaves

PILUM: a heavy javelin 5 to 7 feet long

PUGIO: dagger
SCUTUM: wooden shield with brass edging

Terrorist Organizations, 2003

Designated by the U.S. Department of State.

Abu Nidal Organization (ANO)
Abu Sayyaf Group
Al-Aqsa Martyrs Brigade
al-Jihad (Egyptian Islamic Jihad)
Al Qa'ida
Armed Islamic Group (GIA)
Asbat al-Ansar
Aum Shinrikyo
Basque Fatherland and Liberty (ETA)
Communist Party of the Philippines/New People's Army (CPP/NPA)
Gama'a al-Islamiyya (Islamic Group)
HAMAS (Islamic Resistance Movement)
Harakat ul-Mujahidin (HUM)
Hizbollah (Party of God)
Islamic Movement of Uzbekistan (IMU)
Jaish-e-Mohammed (JEM) (Army of Mohammed)
Jemaah Islamiya Organization (JI)
Kahane Chai (Kach)
Kurdistan Workers' Party (PKK) a.k.a. Kurdistan Freedom and
    Democracy Congress (KADEK)
Lashkar-e Tayyiba (LT) (Army of the Righteous)
Lashkar i Jhangvi
Liberation Tigers of Tamil Eelam (LTTE)
Mujahedin-e Khalq Organization (MEK)
National Liberation Army (ELN)
Palestinian Islamic Jihad (PIJ)
Palestine Liberation Front (PLF)

Popular Front for the Liberation of Palestine (PFLP)
PFLP-General Command (PFLP-GC)
Real IRA
Revolutionary Armed Forces of Colombia (FARC)
Revolutionary Nuclei (formerly ELA)
Revolutionary Organization 17 November
Revolutionary People's Liberation Army/Front (DHKP/C)
Salafist Group for Call and Combat (GSPC)
Shining Path (Sendero Luminoso, SL)
United Self-Defense Forces of Colombia (AUC)

The Loads They Carried

Weight of personal weapons and equipment.

Roman legionary under Marius, first century B.C.—66 pounds
Armored French knight at Agincourt, 1415—80 pounds
Union soldier at Gettysburg, 1863—50 pounds
World War I American doughboy, 1917—48 pounds
Allied infantryman on D-day, 1944—80 pounds
Russian soldier during the advance on Berlin, 1945—40 pounds
British Royal Marine in the Falklands, 1982—120 pounds
U.S. Army soldier on patrol in Afghanistan, 2002—100 pounds

The Payloads They Carried

Aircraft and their maximum bomb loads.

Zeppelin VGO I Airship (1915), Germany—2,200 pounds
Boeing B-17 Flying Fortress (1935), United States—4,000 pounds
Avro Lancaster (1942), Great Britain—14,000 pounds
Boeing B-52 Stratofortress (1955), United States—60,000 pounds
Avro Vulcan (1956), Great Britain—21,000 pounds

Tu-160 Blackjack (1981), U.S.S.R.—36,000 pounds
Rockwell B-1 Lancer (1985), United States—75,000 pounds
Northrop Grumman B-2 Spirit (1993), United States—40,000
  pounds

Roman Legion Organization

  1 Contubernium = 8 men
10 Contubernia = 1 Century (80 men)
  2 Centuries = 1 Maniple (160 men)
  6 Centuries = 1 Cohort (480 men)
10 Cohorts and 120 horsemen = 1 Legion
    (5,240 men, including one extra-strength First Cohort)

Spears Against Rifles

Defeats of Western armies by native forces.

1. SUDAN, 1883: The "Mad Mahdi" and his dervishes massacred a force of 10,000 British troops under William Hicks.
2. ISANDLWHANA, 1879: 1,300 British and allied troops were wiped out by 20,000 Zulu warriors.
3. LITTLE BIGHORN, 1876: George Armstrong Custer and 264 men of the 7th Cavalry were slaughtered to the last man by Sioux Indian braves.
4. FLORIDA, 1816–42: The Seminole Indians were the only tribe never to be defeated by the U.S. Army. Holding out in the Everglades, they resisted forcible relocation to Mississipi and cost the government $20 million and 1,500 lives in two wars (1817–18 and 1835–42).

Sticks Against Swords

Defeats of Roman legions by ancient barbarians.

1. THE SACK OF ROME BY CELTIC GAULS, 390 B.C.: The citizenry was alerted to the attack by the honking of the sacred geese of Juno, presaging a seven-month siege.
2. THE BATTLE OF ALLIA, 386 B.C.: The Roman army was routed by Gallic chieftain Brennus on the banks of the River Allia, north of Rome. Thereafter July 18 was regarded as unlucky.
3. THE TEUTOBURGIAN FOREST, A.D. 9: Three Roman legions under Quintilius Varus were slaughtered by Goths under Armininius, with survivors sacrificed to the barbarian gods and Varus's severed head sent to Roman leaders in the south.
4. THE ADRIANOPLE CAMPAIGN, 376–378: In 378, the emperor Valens and 40,000 troops were slaughtered by the Goths at Adrianople.
5. THE SACK OF ROME BY ALARIC'S VISIGOTHS, 410.

War Ruses

Great Deceptions of World War II.

THE MAN WHO NEVER WAS: On April 30, 1943, a British submarine released off the Spanish coast a body dressed as an officer of the Royal Marines. Affixed to the corpse's wrist was an attaché case containing papers giving him the fictitious name Major Martin and fake plans for the invasion of Greece. The information was passed onto a credulous Adolf Hitler via the German consul, thereby ensuring that the attack on Sicily was unexpected.

THE 'BURBS OF BURBANK: Hollywood set designers constructed an entire American suburb—complete with canvas houses, cars, trees, washing lines, and the painted continuation of local roads—which was draped over the giant aircraft factory at Burbank, California, to defy Japanese spotter planes. Stories circulated on both sides of dummy airfields being attacked with wooden bombs.

THE MAGNIFICENT MASKELYNE: The famous stage magician Jasper Maskelyne invented canvas covers for tanks to make them look like trucks and inflatable submarines and battleships to confuse enemy reconnaissance. In 1941 he manufactured a simulacrum of the port of Alexandria, complete with lighthouse, which was lit up every night several miles down the coast from the actual city to decoy German bombers.

Some Military Theorists

SUN TZU (FIRST HALF OF FIFTH CENTURY B.C.): Author of *The Art of War.* Based on the premise that war is an evil, this is probably the best book on military strategy ever written.

AENEAS THE TACTICIAN (MID-THIRD CENTURY B.C.): Greek author of the earliest work on military tactics. Of his oeuvre, only *On Siegecraft* survives.

ASCLEPIODOTUS (FIRST CENTURY B.C.): Wrote *Outline of Tactics,* an essay containing a discussion of the structure of the Greek phalanx.

ONASANDER (MID-FIRST CENTURY A.D.): Writer of *The General,* a treatise on military psychology and tactics.

SEXTUS JULIUS FRONTINUS (LATE FIRST CENTURY A.D.): His *Strategemata,* a compendium of military ruses, was famous throughout the Middle Ages.

ARRIAN (86–160): Writer of textbooks on Greek and Roman military drill, including *Ektasis (Order of March).*

VEGETIUS (LATE FOURTH CENTURY A.D.): His *Epitoma Rei Militaris (Epitome of Military Science)* covered all aspects of warfare from recruitment and training to naval combat.

EMPEROR MAURICE (C. 600): Supposed author of *Strategikon*, a guide to all aspects of the Byzantine army of the seventh century.

JEAN DE BUEIL (C. 1410–70): Author of *Le Jouvencel*, a treatise on warfare as a political tool that predated Machiavelli's better-known work.

NICCOLÒ MACHIAVELLI (1469–1527): Author of *The Art of War* and, more famously, *The Prince*.

CHEVALIER FOLARD (1669–1752): Wrote *New Discoveries about War* and coined the phrase "fog of war."

CARL VON CLAUSEWITZ (1780–1831): Prussian general and author of the justly famous *On War*, stressing the political psychology of warfare and the importance of logistics.

ALFRED THAYER MAHAN (1840–1914): American naval historian and strategist who wrote *The Influence of Sea Power Upon History, 1660–1783,* advocating sea power as a determinant of the nation's strength.

J. F. C. FULLER (1876–1966): British pioneer of tank warfare.

HEINZ GUDERIAN (1888–1954): Writer of *Achtung Panzer!,* a development of the ideas of Fuller and Liddell Hart.

BASIL LIDDELL HART (1895–1970): Claimed to be the inventor of blitzkrieg tactics, which were ignored by the British authorities but taken up with enthusiasm in Germany.

MAO TSE-TUNG (1893–1976): Condensed the experience of the Long March into *On Guerrilla Warfare* (1937).

Military Orders

The Christian soldiers of the Middle Ages.

1. THE KNIGHTS TEMPLAR: Authorized by the papacy in 1128 to protect pilgrims on their way to bathe in the River Jordan. In 1307 their assets were seized by Philip IV of France, and their last Grand Master was burned for heresy in 1314.

2. THE HOSPITALLERS OF ST. JOHN OF JERUSALEM: Founded to look after sick pilgrims, they became a military order in the mid-twelfth century. They ruled the island of Rhodes from 1306 to 1480, when they were expelled by the Turks. They retreated to Malta, which they fortified well enough to resist Suleiman the Magnificent's invasion of 1565, but were eventually defeated by Napoleon in 1798 after years of decay.

3. THE TEUTONIC KNIGHTS: Amalgamated in 1212 from several Baltic orders, they ruled the region until their defeat by the Poles at Tannenberg in 1410.

4. THE ORDER OF OUR LADY OF RANSOM: Founded in Aragon in 1218 by St. Peter Nolasco for the redemption of captured crusaders.

5. THE SWORDBEARERS: Short-lived order founded by Albert, first bishop of Riga, in 1197 for the conversion of Baltic pagans. Populated by adventurers rather than the pious, it was absorbed by the Teutonic Knights in 1238.

Northern Irish Paramilitary Groups

IRA—Irish Republican Army (Republican)

PIRA—Provisional Irish Republican Army, formed after official IRA declared a cease-fire in 1972 (Republican)

RIRA—Real IRA, formed after PIRA declared a cease-fire in 1997 (Republican)

CIRA—Continuity IRA, attracted members from RIRA when that organization declared a cease-fire in 1998 (Republican)

INLA—Irish National Liberation Army (Republican)

SDA—Shankhill Defence Association (Loyalist)

UVF—Ulster Volunteer Force (Loyalist)

LVF—Loyalist Volunteer Force (Loyalist)

UDA—Ulster Defence Association (Loyalist)

UFF—Ulster Freedom Fighters (Loyalist), cover name for the UDA

RHD—Red Hand Defenders (Loyalist). Possibly does not exist, being only a cover under which UVF and UDA members can carry out acts of violence without breaking their cease-fire agreements.

"Sod 'em All"

Allied soldiers' ditty from World War II, sung to the tune of "Bless 'em All."

> Sod 'em all. Sod 'em all,
> The long and the short and the tall,
> Sod all the sergeants and WO1s,
> Sod all the corporals and their bastard sons,
> For we're saying good-bye to them all,
> As back to their billets they crawl,
> You'll get no promotion
> This side of the ocean,
> So cheer up, my lads, sod 'em all.

Notable Fortifications

1. THE WALLS OF JERICHO: Now called the Tel es-Sultan in Jordan, the neolithic city possessed the earliest known stone walls and tower. Remains of the city date to the eighth millennium B.C.
2. THE GREAT WALL OF CHINA: Begun by the emperor Qin Shi Huangdi in 214 B.C. for defense against marauding nomad horsemen, the wall extends 4,000 miles westward from Po Hai on the Yellow Sea. It is one of only two man-made constructions reputedly visible from outer space (the other being New York City's Staten Island garbage dump).
3. THE LONG WALLS OF ATHENS: Two parallel walls built to form a protected corridor a hundred miles wide between Ancient

Athens and the port of Piraeus that was essential for its supply in times of siege. Each was 6,500 miles long.

4. HADRIAN'S WALL: Built across northern Britain by the Roman emperor Hadrian, the 5.9-foot-thick wall ran 68 miles from Bowness on the Solway Firth to Wallsend on the River Tyne. Fortified gateways ("milecastles") were located every Roman mile (1,618 yards).

5. THE DANEVIRKE: This 12-mile rampart and ditch was built across the base of the Jutland Peninsula around the year 800.

6. THE ORDOS LOOP WALL: Built toward the end of the fifteenth century across the Ordos loop of the Yellow River to prevent Mongol attacks, it was about 650 miles long and included 800 forts and towers.

7. THE HINDENBURG LINE: German World War I line of western fortifications constructed between 1916 and 1917, most of which were not breached until the British summer offensive of 1918.

8. THE MAGINOT LINE: Between 1929 and 1940, France built a line of concrete fortifications, tank traps, and machine-gun posts supported by a network of bunkers and 60 miles of tunnels to guard against any future German invasion. In 1940, Hitler's troops bypassed these defenses by going through Belgium, the Netherlands, and the supposedly impassable Ardennes Forest.

9. THE SIEGFRIED LINE: Built in the 1930s and strengthened later, this was Nazi Germany's last line of defense against the Western Allies. Also known as the West Wall, it ranged from heavily protected forts to "dragon's teeth" tank obstacles and was not breached until the spring of 1945.

10. THE BERLIN WALL: Built in 1961 by the communist authorities to prevent East Germans from escaping to freedom into West Berlin.

11. HASSAN'S WALL: The late Moroccan king Hassan II built a wall of fortified rubble and razor wire more than 1,000 miles long to protect his occupation of the western Sahara after his

1975 invasion. Morocco spends $2 million a day maintaining the wall and its occupying forces—paid for by the exploitation of western Saharan oil wealth.

Napoleon's Marshals

Augereau	Jourdan	Murat
Bernadotte	Kellermann	Ney
Berthier	Lannes	Oudinot
Bessières	Lefebvre	Perignon
Brune	Macdonald	Poniatowski
Clauzel	Marmont	Schet
Davout	Masséna	Serurier
Gouvion St-Cyr	Moncey	Soult
Grouchy	Mortier	Victor

Top Fighter Aces

These figures are much disputed even today.
What follows are best estimates.

First World War

1. Manfred von Richthofen (the Red Baron), Germany, 80 aircraft downed
2. René Paul Fonck, France, 75
3. William Bishop, Canada, 72
4. Raymond Collishaw, Canada, 62
5. Ernst Udet, Germany, 62

TOP BRITISH ACE: Edward Mannock, 61
TOP UNITED STATES ACE: Edward V. Rickenbacker, 26

Second World War

1. Erich Hartmann, Germany, 352
2. Gerhard Barkhorn, Germany, 301
3. Guenther Rall, Germany, 275
4. Otto Kittel, Germany, 267
5. Walter Nowotny, Germany, 258

TOP JAPANESE ACE: Hiroyoshi Nishizawa, 113
TOP RAF ACE: Marmaduke "Pat" Pattle (South African), 40+
TOP RUSSIAN ACE: Ivan Kozhedub, 62
TOP FRENCH ACE: Pierre Clostermann, 33
TOP ITALIAN ACE: Teresio Martinoli, 22
TOP POLISH ACE: Stanislaw Skalski, 22
TOP NORWEGIAN ACE: Sevin Heglund, 14
TOP DUTCH ACE: Gerald Kesseler, 16
TOP HUNGARIAN ACE: Dezso Szentgyorgyi, 34
TOP CZECH ACE: Karel Miroslav Kuttelwascher, 20
TOP CROAT ACE: Mato Dubovak, 40
TOP ROMANIAN ACE: Constantine Cantacuzine, 60
Top female ace of World War II—and of all time—was Lydia
    Litvak of the U.S.S.R. with 12 kills between 1941 and 1943
R. B. Mayne, an SAS soldier, once destroyed 47 Axis planes on
    the ground in one night, more than any Allied fighter ace
    managed during the entire war.

Top American Aces of the Second World War

1. Richard I. Bong, 40
2. Thomas McGuire, 38
3. David McCampbell, 34
4. Francis "Gabby" Gabreski, 28
5. Robert S. Johnson, 27
   Charles MacDonald, 27

6. Joseph Foss, 26 *
    George Preddy, 26
7. Robert M. Hanson, 25
8. John C. Meyer, 24
    Cecil E. Harris, 24

*In January 2002, the eighty-six-year-old Foss was detained and searched by airport security in Phoenix, Arizona, after staff mistook his Congressional Medal of Honor for an offensive weapon and refused to believe that he had received it from President Franklin Roosevelt.

Korean War Aces

1. Nicolai V. Sutyagin, U.S.S.R., 21
2. Yevgeny G. Pepelyaev, U.S.S.R., 19
3. Lev Kirilovich Shchukin, U.S.S.R., 17
4. Joseph McConnell, United States, 16
5. James Jabara, United States, 15

"Ace of Aces" Erich Hartmann on Dogfighting

Once committed to an attack, fly in at full speed. After scoring crippling or disabling hits, I would clear myself and then repeat the process. I never pursued the enemy once they had eluded me. Better to break off and set up again for a new assault. I always began my attacks from full strength, if possible, my ideal flying height being 22,000 feet because at that altitude I could best utilize the performance of my aircraft. Combat flying is based on the slashing attack and rough maneuvring. In combat flying, fancy precision aerobatic work is really not of much use. Instead, it is the rough maneuvre which succeeds.

Notable Special Forces Missions

1. OPERATION CLAYMORE, 1941: A British commando expedition to the Nazi-occupied Lofoten Islands off Norway destroyed eleven factories, 800,000 gallons of oil, and five ships, acquired 314 volunteers for the free Norwegian forces, and captured 60 collaborators, 225 German prisoners, and a set of Enigma code ciphers. The only casualty was one self-inflicted thigh wound.

2. OPERATION OAK, 1943: In July 1943, Mussolini was removed from power by the king of Italy and imprisoned in a Gran Sasso ski hotel, which was accessible only by cable car. In September he was rescued in an airborne raid by German troops led by Otto Skorzeny.

3. OPERATION BRICKLAYER, APRIL 1944: Major General Heinrich Kreipe, commander of Germany's 22nd Infantry Division, was kidnapped from occupied Crete in a commando raid and spirited away by sea.

4. RAID ON ENTEBBE AIRPORT, 1976: A French airliner, hijacked by Palestinian and Baader-Meinhof terrorists, landed in Uganda with the collusion of despot Idi Amin. Israeli special forces flew 2,000 miles to the airport in four Hercules transports and rescued 103 hostages in fifty-three minutes. The Israelis lost only a single soldier, shot in the back by a Ugandan sniper. Three hostages died in the assault, with a fourth later murdered by the Ugandans, while all 7 hijackers, along with 20 Ugandan soldiers, were killed. The commandos also destroyed 7 MiG jet fighters stationed at the airport.

5. MOGADISHU, 1977: The German counterterrorist unit GSG 9 and two British SAS men assaulted a hijacked Lufthansa airliner in Mogadishu in Somalia. Within six minutes, all 87 hostages had been rescued in the "cleanest" special op ever.

6. MOLUCCAN TRAIN INCIDENT, 1977: South Moluccan terrorists took 49 people hostage in a Dutch express train while a group of their comrades took 110 children hostage in an elementary

school (releasing 106). The school hostages were rescued unharmed when Royal Dutch Marines burst through the wall of the building, catching 3 of their captors asleep. The train was assaulted by a second Marine team in a twenty-minute attack while low-flying jet fighters ignited their afterburners overhead to distract the terrorists and keep the hostages' heads down. Two hostages were killed, with 2 marines and 7 hostages wounded.

7. IRANIAN EMBASSY SIEGE, 1980: Six Iranians armed with submachine guns took control of the London embassy in protest to Ayatollah Khomeini's rule. Twenty-six hostages were rescued in eleven minutes by a team of twelve SAS troopers who killed 5 terrorists and captured the survivor.

8. OPERATION ACID GAMBIT, 1989: Robert Muse, an anti-Noriega agitator, was held hostage by the Panamanian regime in a militarized jail under armed guards who were instructed to kill him at the first sign of American aggression against the island. A Delta Force team entered through the roof, killed or bound the guards (depending on whether or not they resisted), and rescued Muse with no losses, though two helicopters were shot down. Muse's bodyguard, despite having been hit in the head by a rotor blade, fended off enemy attacks until a U.S. Army unit relieved the special forces.

9. SIERRA LEONE, 2000: SAS and British paratroopers rescued 7 hostages from the West Side Boys armed militia in their jungle encampment. In an action that broke the West Side Boys as a force in the country, one of the rescuers was killed and one seriously wounded, while 25 militia men were killed and 18 captured, including the leader.

Special Forces Disasters

1. CYPRUS TRAGEDY, 1978: Egypt's TF777 special forces rescued 30 hostages from Arab terrorists claiming to represent the PLO in Nicosia, Cyprus. After completing the mission, 15 of their

number were shot dead by Cypriot National Guardsmen who mistook them for more terrorists, claiming that the Egyptian government had not forewarned them of the mission.

2. OPERATION EAGLE CLAW, 1980: After a group of Iranians took 53 men and women hostage in the U.S. embassy in Tehran, a plan was devised under which a Delta Force team would land outside the capital in helicopters, make their way to the embassy, rescue the hostages, and fight their way through a city of 6 million people to the airport, from where they would be flown out. The mission was aborted when one helicopter broke down en route and two collided in a dust storm, killing 8 servicemen. One hostage later remarked, "Thank God they never got here."

3. MALTA FIASCO, 1985: Palestinian terrorists hijacked an Egyptian Boeing 737, forcing it to land in Luqa, Malta. Lacking a plan of the internal layout of their own national carrier's aircraft, Egyptian special forces first blew a hole in the roof, killing 20 passengers in the rows beneath. They then burst into the cabin, firing wildly and hurling high-explosive grenades. Passengers who managed to escape from the melee were mistaken for terrorists by TF777 troopers waiting outside and were shot down as they ran to safety. A total of 57 hostages died.

4. AFGHANISTAN, 2001: A U.S. special forces soldier protecting the newly invested Afghan leader Hamid Karzai gave his own GPS coordinates to a B-52 bomber crew rather than those of a Taliban position. Karzai received only light wounds, but 23 Afghans and 3 Americans were killed.

5. MOSCOW THEATER SIEGE, 2002: When some 800 people were taken hostage by Chechen rebels in a Moscow theater, Russian special forces pumped an unnamed gas into the building before their assault to incapacitate the terrorists and 116 hostages died from the effects of the chemicals.

Know Your Enemy

Admiral Yamamoto Isoroku's advice to junior officers of the Japanese Imperial Navy, 1939.

You can tell a man's character by the way he makes advances to a woman. Men like you, for example, when the fleet's in port and you go off to have a good time, you seem to have only two ways of going about things. First, you put it straight to the woman: "Hey, how about a lay?" Now, any woman, even the lowest whore, is going to put up at least a show of refusing if she's asked like that. So what do you do next? You either act insulted and get rough, or you give up immediately and go off and try the same thing on the next woman. That's all you're capable of. But take a look at Western men—they're quite different. Once they've set their sights on a woman, they invite her out for a drink, or to dinner, or to go dancing. In that way they gradually break down her defenses until, in the end, they get what they want, and in style at that. Where achieving a particular aim is concerned, that's surely a far wiser way of going about things. At any rate, they're the kind of men you'd be dealing with if it were a war, so you'd better give it some thought.

Famous Marches

1. THE MARCH OF THE TEN THOUSAND: A Greek mercenary force of veterans from the Peloponnesian War was hired by Cyrus the Younger to aid his rebellion against his elder brother in Persia. After Cyrus was killed at Cunaxa in 401 B.C., the Greeks were forced to fight their way home in an action that became legendary for both their victories on the battlefields as they retreated and the atrocities they inflicted on neighboring populations.

2. HAROLD'S MARCH NORTH: In 1066, Harold Godwinson's Saxon army covered 190 miles to Tadcaster, near York, in less than five days. After defeating Harald Hardrada's Viking invasion force at Stamford Bridge on September 25, Harold's army had to march back again, reaching London on October 5, to face William and the Normans on the south coast. The exertion almost certainly contributed to their defeat at Hastings.

3. CHIEF JOSEPH'S RETREAT: After war broke out in Idaho in 1877 between the Nez Percé tribe and white settlers, Joseph led his followers on a retreat across over a thousand miles of mountainous terrain to reach the safety of Canada. However, they were intercepted by the U.S. Army only thirty miles from the border and were forced to surrender.

4. THE LONG MARCH: In 368 days from 1934–35, 90,000 Chinese communists under Mao Tse-Tung marched 6,000 miles from Kiangsi to Yenan via Yunnan. Twenty-two thousand survived the journey and the continual attacks from Nationalist forces.

5. THE BATAAN DEATH MARCH: During World War II, 78,000 U.S. POWs were beaten and bayoneted by their Japanese captors and forced to walk 65 miles from Mariveles to San Fernando in the Philippines.

6. THE BIG YOMP: During the Falklands War of 1982, the British troops of 45 Commando marched 80 miles from San Carlos to Port Stanley in three days. Each man carried some 120 pounds of equipment through hostile territory in freezing conditions.

The Effects of a One-Megaton Nuclear Airburst

By distance from detonation.

7 MILES: Many severely burned, all outdoors blinded, trees and buildings damaged. Winds reach 35mph.

5 MILES: Most people severely burned, all outdoors blinded, trees blown down. Winds reach 95mph.

4 MILES: Many dead from radiation, all outdoors blinded, most buildings damaged. Winds reach 160mph.

3 MILES: Most people dead from burns, all outdoors blinded, all houses destroyed, all larger buildings damaged. Winds reach 290mph.

2 MILES: All people killed, all buildings destroyed. Winds reach 470mph.

The Haka

The Maori prebattle chant now used by the New Zealand All Blacks rugby team before matches.

Ka Mate! Ka Mate!	It is death! It is death!
Ka Ora! Ka Ora!	It is life! It is life!
Tenei te ta ngata puhuru huru	This is the hairy person
Nana nei i tiki mai	Who caused the sun to shine
Whakawhiti te ra	Keep abreast! Keep abreast!
A upane ka upane!	The rank! Hold fast!
A upane kaupane whiti te ra!	Into the sun that shines!
Hi!!	

Ten of the Bloodiest Battles

1. STALINGRAD, 1942–43: Approximately 300,000 German troops and 500,000 Soviet soldiers perished in Hitler's battle for the strategic industrial city on the Volga River.

2. THE KURSK SALIENT, 1943: In a series of engagements, including the largest tank battle in history, Germany suffered upwards of 70,000 casualties. The Soviet victors sustained some one million casualties.

3. THE FIRST BATTLE OF THE SOMME, 1916: Between July 1 and November 13, approximately 650,000 Germans, 420,000 British,

and 195,000 French became casualties. The British suffered 57,470 casualties on the first day alone, with an entire battalion— the 10th West Yorks—virtually annihilated within a minute of their advance.

4. THE THIRD BATTLE OF YPRES, JULY 31–NOVEMBER 6, 1917: 325,000 Allied and 260,000 German troops became casualties at Passchendaele as Douglas Haig's offensive foundered under the heaviest rains in thirty years. The Germans regained most of their lost territory the following April.

5. VERDUN, 1916: Nearly 160,000 French troops died in the German assault on Verdun and the town's screen of forts along the Meuse River. German losses are thought to have been almost as high. By the end of the year, the French had recovered most of their ground.

6. THE BATTLE OF THE BULGE, 1944–45: Between December 16 and January 25, Hitler's surprise counterattack through the Ardennes inflicted some 81,000 casualties on the Americans. However, the attack was blunted and the Germans suffered more than 100,000 losses of their own.

7. OKINAWA, 1945: 12,000 Americans and 100,000 Japanese died in the struggle for the island.

8. BORODINO, SEPTEMBER 7, 1812: In eleven hours of fighting, described in Tolstoy's *War and Peace,* Napoleon lost 30,000 men and the Russians 45,000. The victory enabled Napoleon to enter Moscow unopposed, but enough Russians survived to bring about his eventual defeat.

9. GETTYSBURG, JULY 1–3, 1863: The bloodiest engagement on American soil resulted in 51,112 casualties (23,049 Union and 28,063 Confederate). The most casualties in a single day during the U.S. Civil War were suffered at Antietam on September 17, 1862, with 12,410 Union and 13,724 Confederate losses.

10. TOWTON, 1461: The most costly engagement on British soil took place during the Wars of the Roses. Total casualties in the Yorkist victory reached near 20,000.

Seven Bloodless Battles

1. THE SIEGE OF SEVILLE: In 1078 King Alfonso VI of Castile prepared for a siege to drive out the Moors. When the Moorish ruler Al-Mutamid heard that Alfonso was a chess enthusiast, he sent his chess champion, Ibn-Ammar, to play a game with the king for possession of the city. Ibn-Ammar won and the Castilians withdrew.

2. THE BATTLE OF BRÉMULE: On August 20, 1119, 900 English and French knights fought a pitched battle that resulted in only three deaths.

3. THE RECAPTURE OF CONSTANTINOPLE: In 1261 the Western Crusaders who had brought the city within the Latin empire in 1204 left it undefended while their fleet was at sea, allowing 500 Byzantine troops under Alexios to walk through the gates.

4. THE RECOVERY OF JERUSALEM: Frederick II led a crusade to the city in 1229 but won it though entreaty.

5. THE CAPTURE OF MOSCOW: On September 14, 1812, Napoleon took an undefended, emptied, and burning city. The emperor himself was rescued from the blazing Kremlin by French looters and began the famous retreat on October 19.

6. THE MOCK BATTLE OF MANILA: On August 13, 1898, General Jaudenes, the Spanish commander of the city's garrison, knew that his position was hopeless. However, to avoid the dishonor of surrendering to an American invasion force without a fight, he and Admiral Dewey choreographed an invasion whereby the Spanish would abandon successive sections of their defenses according to signals flagged by the Americans.

7. THE BATTLE OF THE PIPS: "The pips" refers to those who appeared on the radar screen of a U.S. flying boat off the Aleutian Islands in July 1943. Taken for a Japanese supply convoy, warships were sent to intercept. More radar signals led to an attack in which a thousand shells were fired, while seamen reported seeing flares, lights, and the wakes of torpedoes narrowly missing their vessels. Those belowdecks felt the shock of explosions,

while one sailor suffered a nervous breakdown "under fire." The pips were subsequently identified as the echoes from mountains a hundred miles away.

Friendly Fire Incidents

1. Confederate General Stonewall Jackson was mistakenly and fatally shot by three of his own troops after the Confederate triumph at Chancellorsville in 1863.
2. In his first engagement during World War I, Lawrence of Arabia shot his own camel in the back of the head.
3. Over the course of World War I, some 75,000 French troops were killed by their own artillery. The Germans suffered similar problems, their 49th Artillery Regiment rechristened the 48½th for persistently firing short.
4. On September 24, 1915, in retaliation for German use of poison gas, 400 chlorine gas emplacements were established along the British front lines around Loos. After the gas was released, the wind changed direction in the most northerly sector, blowing it back into the British trenches. Elsewhere, the gas was effective.
5. Italy's Marshal Italo Balbo, Mussolini's commander in Libya, was shot down by his own antiaircraft defenses at Tobruk in 1940.
6. The highest-ranking American to die in World War II was Lieutenant General Lesley McNair, killed by a stray bomb dropped by the U.S. Army Air Corps.
7. Following a massive naval bombardment of the Aleutian island of Kiska in June 1943, 35,000 U.S. and Canadian troops stormed ashore. Twenty-one troops were killed in the firefight before it was found there were no Japanese forces on the island.
8. A German ship used to intern Allied POWs lay anchored off Cape Bon for three days in May 1943. During that time, it was strafed and bombed by forty Allied aircraft. Poor shooting meant that only one POW was killed, with just a single bomb out of 100—a dud—hitting its target.

9. In Vietnam in 1967, a U.S. artillery unit selected the wrong powder charges for its ordnance, resulting in the shells falling on an American base camp, killing one and wounding thirty-seven. Believing they were under enemy attack, the gunners at the camp returned fire and during a thirty-three minute battle a further twelve were killed and forty wounded.

10. Fragging—In 1969, there were 126 incidents of American troops in Vietnam turning on their own officers, often by rolling a grenade into their tent. Thirty-seven men died as a result. In 1971 there were 333 incidents, resulting in twelve fatalities.

11. A total of 35 of the 148 U.S. combat deaths in the 1991 Persian Gulf War were self-inflicted. A further 78 U.S. soldiers were wounded by their comrades, making friendly fire responsible for 17 percent of all American casualties. Of the British troops involved in the conflict, nine were killed by U.S. forces and only seven by the Iraqis.

Sacked Cities

1. THE CONQUEST OF KALINGA (NOW THE INDIAN STATE OF ORISSA), 261 B.C.: After more than 100,000 of the region's inhabitants were killed by his invasion, the victorious but horrified Indian emperor Ashoka renounced violence and became a Buddhist.

2. THE FALL OF CARTHAGE, 146 B.C.: From a population of 200,000, only 50,000 survived to be enslaved by Scipio Aemilianus's Romans.

3. BERWICK, 1296: King Edward I of England, the Hammer of the Scots, spent three days slaughtering almost every adult, child, and animal in the town. He eventually called off the massacre when he saw his men hacking a pregnant woman to death; 7,000 to 8,000 were killed.

4. KABUL, 1843: During their retreat from Kabul, 4,500 British and Indian soldiers and their families, together with 10,000 Afghans, attempted to flee the city and escape Dost Mohammed's forces. Only one man made it to the Indian border alive.

5. THE SACK OF NANKING, 1864: Government forces killed more than 100,000 people in three days during the T'ai-p'ing Rebellion.

6. THE RAPE OF NANKING, 1937: 20,000 women between the ages of ten and seventy were gang-raped by Japanese soldiers. Upwards of 200,000 men were executed.

7. LIDICE, 1942: Five days after the assassination of Deputy Gestapo Chief Reinhard Heydrich, the Czech village of Lidice was chosen at random for retaliation. The 172 men and boys over the age of sixteen were shot and the women and children were separated and sent to concentration camps. Every building in the village was then torched and dynamited, with the remains bulldozed and then covered over with earth and concrete. Finally, new maps of the area were printed from which Lidice was excised.

8. ORADOUR-SUR-GLANE, 1944: When the SS Das Reich Division, rumored to be carrying gold bullion to Normandy, was ambushed by the French Resistance, the nearby Oradour-sur-Glane became the arbitrary target for reprisals. On June 10 the division entered the town and turned the inhabitants out of their homes. The men were taken away and shot, with many surviving to be burned alive. The women and children were locked in the local church, where a gas bomb was detonated. SS troops then entered with machine guns and grenades before finishing off the survivors by covering them with wood and kindling and setting it alight. Afterward, the town was scoured for anyone who had been missed: an invalid was burned in his bed and a baby, possibly hidden there, was roasted to death in a baker's oven. Six hundred and forty-two people died.

Assyrian Boasting

THE DESTRUCTION OF BABYLON: "I leveled the city and its houses from the foundations to the top; I destroyed them and consumed them with fire. I tore down and removed the outer and inner walls, the temples and the ziggurats made of brick, and dumped the rubble in the Arahtu canal. And after I destroyed Babylon, smashed its gods and massacred its population, I tore up its soil and threw it into the Euphrates so that it was carried by the river down to the sea."

—SENNACHERIB OF ASSYRIA, 680 B.C.

THE FIRING OF NIRBI: "The city was exceedingly strong and was surrounded by three walls. The men trusted in their mighty walls and in their hosts, and did not come down, and did not embrace my feet. With battle and slaughter I stormed the city and captured it. Three thousand of their warriors I put to the sword; their spoil and their possessions, their cattle and their sheep I carried off. Many captives from among them I burned with fire, and many I took as living captives. From some I cut off their hands and their fingers, and from others I cut off their noses, their ears and their fingers, of many I put out the eyes. I made one pillar of the living, and another of heads, and I bound their heads to posts round about the city. Their young men and maidens I burned in the fire, the city I destroyed, I devastated, I burned it with fire and consumed it. At that time the cities of the land of Nirbi and their strong walls I destroyed, I devastated, I burned with fire."

—ASSUR-NÂSIR-PAL II, 883–859 B.C.

Frontline Luxuries

1. PROSTITUTES: Napoleon introduced licensed brothels to tackle the gonorrhea and syphilis rampant in the Grande Armée. The principle of forced medical inspections was enshrined in the Napoleonic Code of 1810, and authorized prostitutes serviced

the French army—and, occasionally, its allies—until the mid-1950s. It is rumored that two prostitutes were awarded medals for servicing an isolated garrison in the French Indo-China War of 1947–54.

2. ABSINTHE: Issued to French soldiers in Algeria from 1844 to 1847 as a preventative for malaria.

3. "COMFORT WOMEN": During the 1930s, some 200,000 Korean women were forced to work as sex slaves for the Japanese Imperial Army.

4. SAUNAS: Enjoyed by Finnish troops only 100m behind the front lines during the Russo-Finnish Winter War of 1939.

5. GOURMET COFFEE: Each Italian trooper in North Africa during World War II carried his own personal espresso maker.

6. TWENTY CIGARETTES A DAY: Supplied to U.S. troops in the Pacific theater during World War II.

7. FAST FOOD: Burger King and Pizza Hut opened franchises for U.S. troops waiting to invade of Iraq in 2003.

Meals Ready-to-Eat (MREs)

The twenty-four combat rations currently available to U.S. servicemen.

Beefsteak w/mushrooms and western beans
Jamaican pork chop w/noodles and spiced apples
Beef ravioli with potato sticks
Country captain chicken with buttered noodles
Grilled chicken breast and minestrone stew
Chicken w/thai sauce and white rice
Chicken w/salsa and Mexican rice
Beef patty with nacho cheese pretzels
Beef stew
Chili and macaroni
Pasta w/vegetables in tomato sauce

Bean and rice burrito
Cheese tortellini
Pasta w/vegetables in Alfredo sauce
Beef enchiladas with Mexican rice
Chicken w/noodles
Beef teriyaki with chow mein noodles
Turkey breast w/gravy and potatoes
Beef w/mushrooms and wild rice pilaf
Spaghetti w/meat sauce
Chicken tetrazzini
Jambalaya
Chicken w/cavatelli
Meat loaf w/gravy and mashed potatoes

Drugs Given to Soldiers

1. VIKINGS ON MUSHROOMS: The Norse Berzerker warriors of the Middle Ages are thought to have eaten hallucinogenic fungi to induce battle rage.
2. GERMANS ON COKE: In 1883 Theodor Aschenbrandt administered cocaine to members of the Bavarian army. It was found that the drug enhanced their endurance on maneuvers.
3. TOMMIES ON SPIRITS: British troops were often given an extra ration of rum before an advance during World War I.
4. PARATROOPERS ON BENZEDRINE: Given to German airborne troops dropped into Crete in 1941.
5. GIS ON ACID: In 1957, one thousand American servicemen, who volunteered to test gas masks at the Army Chemical Warfare Laboratories, were instead given doses of LSD to measure the drug's effects.
6. PILOTS ON SPEED: The U.S. Air Force issues what it calls "go pills" to personnel on extended missions. According to U.S. Air Force investigators these amphetamines had been taken by the two pilots who bombed a squad of Canadian infantrymen on a

nighttime exercise in Afghanistan in 2002, killing four and in-
juring eight.

One-Man Armies

1. ORATIUS: The Roman sentry on the Tiber Bridge who in 508
   B.C. held off the Etruscan army single-handedly, long enough
   for his comrades to destroy the crossing.
2. CHORSAMANTIS THE AVAR: During the siege of Rome in
   538, the warrior became maddened by drink and wounds and
   rode out alone to the barbarian camp. He was confronted by
   twenty enemy horsemen, whom he dispatched before being
   overwhelmed.
3. THE LONE VIKING: In 1066, Harold Godwinson's Saxon army
   marched to York to fight off Harald Hardrada's Norwegian invasion. Harold caught his enemies by surprise, but had to
   cross Stamford Bridge to get to them. However, the bridge
   was held by a single Viking champion who slew the first forty
   men who tried to advance. By the time a boat had been floated
   under the bridge and a long spear thrust upward through the
   planks to kill him, the warrior had given his comrades enough
   time to ready their arms and armor and prepare their battle
   formations.
4. BENKEI (DIED 1189): The Japanese warrior monk stood on the
   Gojo Bridge in Kyoto and challenged all comers. According to
   legend he defeated 999 warriors in single combat before being
   beaten.
5. SIR WILLIAM MARSHAL (1146–1219): By common consent the
   greatest warrior of his age. His first engagement was the Battle
   of Drincourt in 1167 where, though his warhorse was killed
   beneath him, he managed to defeat an estimated forty other
   knights in succession without pause.
6. PEDRO FRANCISCO (DIED 1831): The six-foot, six-inch, 280-
   pound Portuguese American was the most famous private soldier

of the American Revolutionary War. In 1779 Francisco captured the British flag at Stony Point, the British army's stronghold on the Hudson River, and during one short engagement killed eleven enemy troops using his six-foot-long broadsword. George Washington said that "Without him we would have lost two crucial battles, perhaps the War, and with it our freedom. He was truly a One-Man Army."

7. JUNIOR J. SPURRIER: The twenty-two-year-old U.S. Infantry staff sergeant was awarded the Congressional Medal of Honor in March 1945 for taking the town of Achain in northern France in a one-man assault. Using grenades, bazookas, heavy machine guns, and his M1 rifle, Spurrier went from house to house, taking strongpoints one by one until he captured the garrison commander and nineteen others, killing twenty-five German soldiers in the process.

8. AUDIE MURPHY (1924–71): Murphy was turned away from the U.S. Marines and the paratroopers for being only five feet, five inches tall yet went on to become the most decorated American soldier of World War II. The engagement for which he won the Medal of Honor took place near Holzwihr in France in January 1945. When his unit was attacked by six German tanks with waves of infantry in support, Murphy ordered his men to retreat into nearby woods while he remained behind to direct artillery fire. When his position was overrun, he climbed onto a burning tank destroyer and held off the enemy with .50-caliber fire. After an hour he had killed or wounded fifty German troops and forced the tanks to retreat. Murphy later enjoyed a successful acting career in Hollywood—playing himself in the 1955 movie of his life, *To Hell and Back*—before dying in a plane crash in 1971.

9. DOUGLAS T. JACOBSON: In a single action during the Battle for Iwo Jima in February 1945, Pfc Jacobson of the US Marines alone wiped out 16 Japanese blockhouses and machine gun positions, a tank and around 75 enemy troops using a bazooka he took from a dead comrade.

10. CHARLES P. MURRAY JR: In December 1944, the U.S. Army first lieutenant was leading a platoon near Kaysersberg in France when he came across a force of 200 Germans who had an American battalion pinned down on a ridge. He crawled ahead of his men to direct artillery fire, but his radio failed. Undeterred, he decided to attack the Germans single-handedly with rifle grenades. Running out of projectiles, he continued his assault with fire from his automatic, killing another twenty enemy soldiers, wounding dozens more, and knocking out a mortar truck. He went on to capture ten Germans in their fox-holes before surviving an explosion from a grenade thrown by an eleventh who had pretended to surrender.

11. LACHHIMAN GURUNG: In May 1945 in Taungdaw, Burma, the Gurkha rifleman was manning the foremost foxhole of his unit's position when 200 Japanese troops attacked. The first two grenades to be thrown into his trench he picked up and threw back, but a third exploded in his right hand, blowing off his fingers, shattering his arm, and permanently blinding him in one eye. For the next four hours, Gurung loaded and fired his rifle with his left arm, killing thirty-one enemy soldiers before the Japanese finally retreated. He remains one of the most celebrated winners of the Victoria Cross.

12. HIROO ONODA: Japanese soldier Lieutenant Onoda refused to stop fighting long after World War II was over, claiming that stories of the war's ending were mere propaganda. It wasn't until March 1974, when his former commanding officer flew out to the remote Pacific island where Onoda was dug in and ordered him to lay down his arms, that he finally complied. However, his record was broken by Private Teruo Nakamura, who maintained his resistance on the island of Morotai for a further nine months until December of 1974.

13. HIROSHI MIYAMURA: The U.S. Army corporal was holding a defensive position during the Korean War in 1953 when communist forces mounted a frontal assault. He bayoneted ten enemy soldiers before returning to his position to administer

first aid to wounded comrades. He then manned a machine gun until his ammunition ran out, whereupon he bayoneted his way through waves of enemies to reach a second gun emplacement. Ordering the other gunners to retreat, he remained behind to cover them, killing a further fifty communists before his ammunition again ran out and he was severely wounded.

Decorations and Awards Won by Audie Murphy, First Lieutenant, Third Infantry Division

The most decorated U.S. soldier of World War II.

Medal of Honor
Distinguished Service Cross
Silver Star with First Oak Leaf Cluster
Legion of Merit
Bronze Star Medal with "V" Device and First Oak Leaf Cluster
Purple Heart with Second Oak Leaf Cluster
U.S. Army Outstanding Civilian Service Medal
Good Conduct Medal
Distinguished Unit Emblem with First Oak Leaf Cluster
American Campaign Medal
European–African–Middle Eastern Campaign Medal with One
    Silver Star
Four Bronze Service Stars (representing nine campaigns)
Bronze Arrowhead (representing assault landing in Sicily and
    southern France)
Second World War Victory Medal
Army of Occupation Medal with Germany Clasp
Armed Forces Reserve Medal
Combat Infantry Badge
Marksman Badge with Rifle Bar
Expert Badge with Bayonet Bar

French Fourragère in colors of the Croix de Guerre
French Legion of Honor, Grade of Chevalier
French Croix de Guerre with Silver Star
French Croix de Guerre with Palm
Medal of Liberated France
Belgian Croix de Guerre 1940 Palm

Great Sea Battles

1. SALAMIS, 480 B.C.: Between 368 and 310 Greek ships commanded by Eurybiades of Sparta defeated some 600 Persian
   vessels by trapping them in the Salamis Strait, where many were
   either outmaneuvred and destroyed or driven ashore.

2. THE ARGINUSAE ISLES, 406 B.C.: In the greatest sea battle of the
   Peloponnesian War, 150 Athenian triremes defeated 120 Spartan
   vessels, sinking 77 with the loss of 25 of their own. However, six
   of the eight Athenian generals involved in the engagement were
   later executed for failing to pick up survivors.

3. AEGOSPOTAMI, 405 B.C.: The final battle of the Peloponnesian
   War, in which the Athenian fleet was destroyed by the Spartans under Lysander.

4. ECNOMUS, 256 B.C.: 330 Roman quinqueremes fought 350
   Carthaginian warships. The day went to the Roman fleet, with
   losses of 24 and 94 respectively.

5. ACTIUM, 31 B.C.: Octavian's 400 ships defeated the combined
   fleets of Mark Antony and Cleopatra with 500 ships. Octavian
   became Augustus, the undisputed ruler of the Roman world.

6. LEPANTO, 1571: 33,000 died in the last great confrontation at
   sea to be fought by galleys. Each side had about 200 ships, the
   Holy League scoring a decisive victory over the Turkish fleet.

7. THE SPANISH ARMADA, 1588: Of the 130 ships that sailed from
   Lisbon to conquer England, only half returned in failure due
   to the attacks of the English fleet in the Channel and storms
   around the coasts of Britain.

8. THE FOUR DAYS' BATTLE, JUNE 1–4, 1666: England's Admiral George Monck with 56 ships engaged Dutch Admiral Michiel de Reuyter's 85 vessels off the North Foreland, Kent. The battle ended only when both sides had run out of ammunition, and although Monck received reinforcements of a further 24 ships on the third, the English suffered a serious defeat, losing 17 ships and 8,000 casualties against the 7 ships and 2,000 casualties suffered by the Dutch.

9. TRAFALGAR, 1805: Admiral Horatio Nelson famously split his 27 warships and attacked Admiral Pierre-Charles Villeneuve's combined French and Spanish fleet of 33 in two squadrons. Though he lost his life to a sniper's bullet, Nelson was rewarded by the capture of 20 French vessels and 2 sunk without any losses to his own force. One of the most decisive battles in history, it put an end to Napoleon's plans to invade Britain.

10. USS *MONITOR* VERSUS THE CSS *MERRIMACK:* The world's first duel between ironclad warships took place in March 1862 and ended in stalemate when neither ship managed to damage its opponent after four hours of combat.

11. JUTLAND, 1916: The largest naval engagement of World War I, in which 151 British ships clashed with 99 German ships in the North Sea. The result was a strategic victory for the British, although they lost 14 ships to the enemy's 11 and suffered more than twice their number of casualties, prompting Admiral Sir David Beatty's remark, "There seems to be something wrong with our bloody ships today."

12. LEYTE GULF, 1944: Over five days and a vast area of sea, 218 American warships supported by 1,280 aircraft engaged 64 Japanese vessels with 716 warplanes in support. Twenty-six Japanese and six American ships were sunk.

Failed Technologies

1. THE BALLONKANONE: The first antiaircraft weapon, a 37mm cannon designed by the Germans to shoot down French balloons during the Siege of Paris in 1870–71. No balloons were shot down.
2. PATRIOT MISSILE: In the Gulf War, 47 Patriots were fired, hitting only a single incoming Scud.
3. MAUS: A giant 192-ton German tank built in 1945 that was too heavy for bridges and soft ground. Despite a 1,200–horsepower engine, its top speed was only 12 mph.
4. FLYING SAUCER: A Canadian firm designed the VZ-9AV Avrocar "flying saucer" for the U.S. Air Force, but the shape proved unstable in flight.
5. MESSERSCHMITT ME 163 KOMET: This German fighter plane was powered by a rocket engine. It was used against Allied bombers from 1944 onward, but its volatile fuel often tended to vaporize the pilot before he could engage enemy aircraft.
6. ROCKWELL XB-70 VALKYRIE: America's Mach-3 bomber was abandoned in 1961 as even at speeds of 1,864 mph it was vulnerable to surface-to-air missiles.
7. THE MITRAILLEUSE: A machine gun thought to be a war-winning weapon by the French was kept so secret that instructions for its use were distributed only on the opening day of the 1870 Franco-Prussian War, by which time they were too late.
8. THE NO. 74 HAND GRENADE: This British explosive was designed to stick to tanks, but it was discontinued after it kept sticking to the hands of its throwers.
9. THE LUNGE BOMB: A Japanese antitank weapon consisting of a grenade on the end of a long spear. The act of placing the weapon in a tank's tracks was usually enough to detonate its charge before the user could retreat to a safe distance.

Rates of Fire Down the Ages

ARQUEBUS / MATCHLOCK MUSKET (FIFTEENTH CENTURY):
2 rounds per minute (rpm)
WHEEL-LOCK MUSKET (SIXTEENTH CENTURY): 2 to 3 rpm
FLINTLOCK MUSKET (SEVENTEENTH CENTURY): 3 rpm
GATLING GUN (1860s): 200 rpm
MAXIM GUN (1880s): 600 rpm
LEE-ENFIELD RIFLE (1900s): 8 rpm
THOMPSON SUBMACHINE GUN (1920s): 725 rpm
BREN GUN (1930s): 500 rpm
M1 GARAND RIFLE (1940s): 24 rpm
KALASHNIKOV AK-47 (1940s): 600 rpm
M16 ASSAULT RIFLE (1950s): 800 rpm
GPMG (1950s): 1,000 rpm
M134 MINIGUN (1960s): 6,000 rpm
SA-80 ASSAULT RIFLE (1980s): 770 rpm
"METAL STORM" (1990s)*: 1,000,000 rpm

*Fired by electronic ignition, with no firing mechanism.

From *The Modern Traveller,* by Hilaire Belloc

> Blood understood the native mind;
> He said we must be firm, but kind.
> A mutiny resulted.
> I never shall forget the way
> That Blood upon this awful day
> Preserved us all from death.
> He stood upon a little mound
> Cast his lethargic eyes around
> And said beneath his breath:
> "Whatever happens we have got
> The Maxim Gun, and they have not."

Big Guns

1. THE GREAT CANNON OF MEHMED: A 42-inch bombard was used by the Turks to attack the walls of Constantinople with 1,200-pound stone balls. Its range was 1 mile but it could be fired only seven times each day.

2. THE TSAR PUCHKA: Now on display in the Kremlin, the 40-ton "King of Cannons" was built in the sixteenth century, with a bore of 36.2 inches and a barrel 10 feet long.

3. BIG BERTHA: A 16.53-inch mortar named after the manufacturer Gustav Krupp's wife, this 43-ton gun could fire a 2,200-pound shell over 9 miles. Transported by Daimler-Benz tractors, it took its 200-man crew six hours or more to reassemble it before it was used to destroy the Belgian defenses at Liège during World War I.

4. THE PARIS-GESCHÜTZ ("PARIS GUN"): Built by the Germans to shell the French capital during World War I, it had a range of 80 miles.

5. THE "BOCHEBUSTER": This 18-inch train-mounted howitzer that could fire a 2,500-pound shell up to 22,800 yards was used by the British from 1940 to help defend the Kent coast.

6. GUSTAV: The 31.5-inch gun used by the Germans in the siege of Sebastopol in 1942 could fire a 10,500-pound shell 29 miles. It fired 300 rounds, including 48 in the Crimea, before its barrel was worn out.

7. V3: Built by the Germans in static underground firing tubes for the shelling of London. Never used, its range was 95 miles.

8. THE IRAQI SUPERGUN: In 1988 construction began of a gun with a 1,000mm bore that could fire a 1,300-pound projectile over 620 miles. Work on the "Babylon Gun" was halted by UN weapons inspectors after the Persian Gulf War of 1991.

Winners of the Dickin Medal for Animal Gallantry

"The Animals' Victoria Cross" instituted by Maria Dickin in 1943.

1. ROB THE "PARADOG": A mongrel that served with the SAS in North Africa in World War II and made twenty-plus parachute jumps.
2. RICKY: A Welsh sheepdog who continued to sniff out landmines despite having one explode in his face in Holland in 1944.
3. GI JOE: An American carrier pigeon that flew 20 miles in 20 minutes just in time to stop a bombing raid on a village that had just been taken, thereby saving up to a hundred Allied lives.
4. ANTIS: A German Alsatian acquired as a puppy from a bombed-out farmhouse by Czech airman Jan Bozdech when he was shot down behind enemy lines during World War II. Antis flew with Bozdech thereafter, and was wounded twice. When Bozdech fell foul of postwar Czechoslovakia's communist authorities and had to flee the country, the dog saved his master's life by savaging a border guard.
5. MARY OF EXETER: A carrier pigeon that flew from 1940 to the end of World War II, surviving three pellets in her body, a wing shot away, two bombing raids on her loft, and an attack by a hawk requiring twenty-two stitches.
6. BEAUTY: A terrier that helped dig out 63 men and women and a cat from under London rubble during the Blitz.
7. SIMON: The ship's cat that served onboard the British escort sloop HMS *Amethyst* in April 1949 in China as Mao Tse-tung's forces took control of the country. When the *Amethyst* was stranded on the Yangtze River and shelled by the Chinese, Simon was trapped in the wreckage for four days. Despite his wounds, he continued to hunt rats and protect the crew's food supply throughout a summer long siege. The story was made into a film, *The Yangtze Incident,* released in 1956.

Nations with the Smallest Armies

1. Costa Rica, none
2. Iceland, none
3. Antigua and Barbuda, 150 troops
4. Seychelles, 450 troops
5. Barbados, 610 troops
6. Luxembourg, 768 troops
7. Gambia, 800 troops
8. Bahamas, 860 troops
9. Belize, 1,050 troops
10. Cape Verde, 1,100 troops

Top French Collaborators

1. MARSHAL HENRI-PHILIPPE PÉTAIN: The Great War hero turned Vichy leader.
2. RUDOLPHE PEUGEOT: Made tanks for Germany until forced by the French Resistance to destroy his factory in order to prevent further Allied bombing of the area.
3. THE MICHELIN FAMILY: Made high-quality tires for the Wehrmacht. The RAF destroyed their factory when they refused to do so themselves.
4. COCO CHANEL: The designer was unrepentant about her relations with Nazi officers, declaring, "My heart is French, but my cunt is international."
5. ROBERT BRASILLACH: Intellectual turned Nazi.

Dogs of War: Mercenaries Past and Present

1. XENOPHON (C. 430–350 B.C.): Greek writer who fought for Cyrus the Younger of Persia in his victorious rebellion against his brother Artaxerxes at the Battle of Cunaxa in 401 B.C.

After Xenophon's employer turned on his allies, he led his fellow Greeks home in a march recounted in his *Anabasis*.

2. THE THREE CAPTAINS: After Carthage's defeat in the First Punic War, she was unable to pay the arrears of her mercenary armies led by Autaritus, Mathos, and Spendius. In the Mercenary War of 241–237 B.C., Tunis was seized, a revolt in Libya incited, and Carthage besieged before the victory of Hamilcar Barca at Bagradas in 240 B.C.

3. MERCADIER: The brutal mercenary ally of Richard the Lionheart became notorious in France for maiming and massacring prisoners of war in the twelfth century.

4. THE CONDOTTIERE: Mercenary companies that formed in the fourteenth century in the wake of the Hundred Years' War and operated in Italy. They included the Catalan Company composed of Catalans, the Grand Company composed of Germans and Hungarians, and the White Company led by the Englishman Sir John Hawkwood.

5. GEORG VON FRUNDSBERG (1473–1528): Called the "Father of the Landsknechts," the Holy Roman Emperor Maximilian I's famous mercenary infantry. Frundsberg won most of Lombardy for Charles V at Bicocca in 1522 and helped defeat the French at Pavia in 1525.

6. GIOVANNI GIUSTINIANI: The mercenary commander who marshaled 7,000 defenders against the 100,000 Turks who besieged Constantinople in 1453. Most of the citizens refused to aid his troops and later suffered for their timidity.

7. THE FLYING TIGERS: American pilots recruited to fight the Japanese in Burma and China in 1941–42. In ten weeks of action over Rangoon, they inflicted 200 losses on superior Japanese forces while losing only 16 of their own aircraft.

8. AIR AMERICA: From 1955 to 1974, CIA-employed pilots flew medevac and reconnaissance missions against the communist insurgents in Laos and transported supplies and troops.

9. BOB DENARD: Denard left the French navy when he was twenty after burning down a restaurant during a drinking bout. He

embarked on a career that took him from Vietnam in the 1940s to the Belgian Congo in the 1960s, when he fought UN troops backing the Zairean leader Patrice Lumumba. Once asked how he could fight for so many different causes, he explained, "I'm not into politics."

10. "MAD" MIKE HOARE: A hard-drinking Irish-born colonel whose exploits in the Congo and South Africa in the 1970s inspired movies such as *The Wild Geese* (1973). In 1982 he was found guilty of hijacking a plane to escape from a failed coup in the Seychelles and sentenced to ten years' imprisonment by a South African court. He and his men had infiltrated the islands disguised as a beer-tasting team called the Ancient Order of Frothblowers.

11. TIM SPICER: London-based Executive Outcomes was hired in 1995 to put down the Revolutionary United Front and keep the peace during the 1996–97 elections in Sierra Leone. A force of 200 South Africans performed the job successfully, but a violent coup followed swiftly when the IMF forced the mercenaries to leave. In 1998, ex-SAS officer Spicer's Sandline Security helped restore the elected president Kabbah while British foreign secretary Robin Cook denied his ministry's involvement.

Target U.S.A.

In June 1942, German U-boats landed two teams of saboteurs in Long Island and Florida as Adolf Hitler launched Operation Pastorius against the United States. All eight agents were captured before they could destroy the following targets using bombs disguised as pieces of coal and blocks of wood:

The Hell Gate Bridge in New York
The Horseshoe Curve railroad track in Pennsylvania
Newark's Penn Station
Great Northern's Cascade Tunnel in Washington

The hydroelectric plants at Niagara Falls
The Aluminium Company of America factories in Illinois,
    Tennessee, and New York
A cryolite plant in Philadelphia
The locks on the Ohio River between Louisville and Pittsburgh
The water supply system for New York City
Jewish-owned stores

The Normandy Beaches

Used in the D-day landings.

Omaha—U.S. landings
Utah—U.S. landings
Juno—Canadian landings
Sword—British landings
Gold—British landings

Code Names for Military Actions

SEA LION: Nazi invasion of Britain initially scheduled for
    September 1940
BARBAROSSA: Hitler's invasion of Russia, 1941
CHASTISE: Dambusters raid, May 1943
HUSKY: Allied invasion of Sicily, 1943
FORTITUDE: Allied plan to deceive Germany that the D-day
    landings of 1944 would take place in Pas de Calais rather than
    Normandy
OVERLORD: Allied invasion of continental Europe, 1944
MARKET GARDEN: Allied airborne and ground attacks through
    Holland, September 1944
ZAPATA: The landings on Cuba's Bay of Pigs, 1961
ROLLING THUNDER: U.S. bombing of North Vietnam, 1965–68

THUNDERBOLT: Israeli commando raid on Entebbe Airport, 1976 (later renamed Operation Jonathan in memory of Jonathan Netanyahu, an officer who died on the mission)

EAGLE CLAW: U.S. attempt to rescue hostages from embassy in Tehran, 1980

CORPORATE: British invasion of the Falklands, 1982

URGENT FURY: U.S. amphibious landings in Grenada, 1983

JUST CAUSE: U.S. invasion of Panama, 1989

DESERT STORM: U.S. and allied action to expel Iraqi forces from Kuwait, 1991

RESTORE HOPE: U.S. peacekeeping in Somalia, 1992

UPHOLD DEMOCRACY: U.S. peacekeeping in Haiti, 1994

DESERT FOX: U.S. and British bombing of Iraq, 1998

ALLIED FORCE: NATO bombing of Serbia and Kosovo, 1999

ENDURING FREEDOM: Allied action against the Taliban in Afghanistan, 2001

IRAQI FREEDOM: U.S. and British invasion of Iraq, 2003

Operation Mongoose

Attempts on the life and reputation of Cuba's President Fidel Castro planned by U.S. agencies.

1. Hiring Mafia hit men to assassinate him.
2. Giving him a scuba-diving outfit infected with tuberculosis.
3. Booby-trapping a seashell that would explode if he lifted it from the seabed while diving.
4. Contaminating his favorite brand of cigars with the untraceable botulinum toxin.
5. Persuading him to write with a poisonous fountain pen.
6. Spiking his drinks with poison.
7. Shooting him with a sniper rifle.
8. Putting a chemical in his shoes that would make his beard fall out.

9. Operation Dirty Trick: A plot to blame Castro if the 1962 Mercury space flight carrying John Glenn crashed.
10. Operation Good Times: Faked photos of an obese Castro with two voluptuous women in a lavishly furnished room and a table laden with fine food. The caption would read, "My ration is different."

Colditz Contraband

Items smuggled to Allied prisoners held in the German castle during World War II by MI9, Britain's escape and evasion service.

1. Railway timetables
2. Information on sentries and frontiers
3. Food ration stamps
4. German currency
5. Maps
6. Compasses
7. Fake identity papers
8. An architect's blueprint of the castle

Methods Used to Attempt Escape from Colditz Castle

1. Walking out of the main gates dressed in German uniform.
2. Dressing in German uniform and "relieving" the sentries on duty.
3. Dressing up as a German housewife.
4. Running off during the daily stroll in the park.
5. Replacing prisoners with dummies while they hid under leaves in the park.
6. Vaulting over the wall.
7. Rappeling from the windows on ropes made from bedsheets.

8. Bribing the guards.
9. Tunneling under the canteen.
10. Hiding inside surplus mattresses sent back to the town.
11. Sliding down the laundry chute.
12. Hiding in the dustcart.
13. Breaking through a lavatory wall.
14. Climbing through a manhole in the park.
15. Digging a tunnel under the chapel.
16. Hiding in the cart used to transport the dug-out earth to the town after the tunnel was discovered.
17. Manufacturing a full-size glider that could be launched from the castle roof carrying two passengers. The castle was liberated before it could be used, but a replica built later worked perfectly.

Bad Predictions

Four or five frigates will do the business without any military force.

—LORD NORTH ON THE AMERICAN REVOLUTION, 1774

No militia will ever acquire the habits necessary to resist a regular force.

—GEORGE WASHINGTON, 1780

The Cavalry will never be scrapped to make room for the tanks; in the course of time Cavalry may be reduced as the supply of horses in this country diminishes. This depends greatly on the life of fox hunting.

—JOURNAL OF THE UNITED SERVICES INSTITUTE, 1921

Some enthusiasts today talk about the probability of the horse becoming extinct and prophesy that the aeroplane, the tank and the motor-car will supersede the horse in future wars. I am sure that as time goes on you will find just as much use for the horse—the well-bred horse—as you have done in the past.

—SIR DOUGLAS HAIG, 1925

People have been talking about a 3,000-mile high-angle rocket shot from one continent to another carrying an atomic bomb, and so directed as to be a precise weapon which would land on a certain target such as this city. I say technically I don't think anybody in the world knows how to do such a thing, and I feel confident it will not be done for a very long period of time to come. I think we can leave that out of our thinking.

—VANNEVAR BUSH, CHIEF U.S. GOVERNMENT SCIENTIST, 1945

You will not need your rifles—all the Germans will be dead in their trenches.

—BRITISH OFFICER AFTER THE ARTILLERY BARRAGE THAT PRECEDED THE BATTLE OF THE SOMME, 1916

My good friends, for the second time in our history, a British Prime Minister has returned from Germany bringing peace with honour. I believe it is "peace for our time." Go home and get a nice quiet sleep.

—NEVILLE CHAMBERLAIN, SEPTEMBER 30, 1938, ON HIS RETURN FROM THE MUNICH CONFERENCE

In three weeks England will have her neck wrung like a chicken.

—MARSHAL PÉTAIN, 1940 (PROMPTING CHURCHILL'S LATER REMARK "SOME CHICKEN! SOME NECK!")

Airplanes are interesting toys but of no military value.

—GENERAL (LATER MARSHAL AND SUPREME COMMANDER OF ALLIED FORCES IN 1918) FERDINAND FOCH, 1911

To throw bombs from an airplane will do as much damage as throwing bags of flour. It will be my pleasure to stand on the bridge of any ship while it is attacked by airplanes.

—NEWTON BAKER, U.S. MINISTER OF DEFENSE, 1921

Even if a submarine should work by a miracle, it will never be used. No country in this world would ever use such a vicious and petty form of warfare.

—WILLIAM HENDERSON, BRITISH ADMIRAL, 1914

Hard pressed on my right; my left is in retreat. My center is yielding. Impossible to maneuvre. Situation excellent. I am attacking.

—GENERAL FERDINAND FOCH TO GENERAL JOSEPH JOFFRE DURING THE BATTLE OF THE MARNE, 1914

You're planning to make a ship sail against wind and tide by lighting a fire below deck? I don't have time to listen to that kind of nonsense.

—NAPOLEON BONAPARTE ON ROBERT FULTON'S PLANS TO MAKE A STEAMBOAT IN THE EARLY NINETEENTH CENTURY.

We should declare war on North Vietnam . . . We could pave the whole country and put parking strips on it, and still be home by Christmas.

—RONALD REAGAN, 1965

Foreign Terms and Phrases

AL QA'IDA: "The Foundation" (Arabic)
ASIBIYA: "The companionship of warriors" (Arabic)
BANZAI: From *Tenno heika banzai* (Long live the emperor)
BLITZKRIEG: "Lightning war" (German)

BUSHIDO: "The way of the warrior" (Japanese)

ESPRIT DE CORPS: "Team spirit" on the battlefield (French)

FEDAYEEN: "Those who sacrifice themselves" (Arabic)

GUERRE COUVERTE: Term for a war involving minor noblemen of the Middle Ages who had the authority to kill and maim but not to take prisoners or damage property (French)

GUERRE DE COURSE: French term for naval warfare directed specifically against a nation's seaborne trade

HO CHI MINH: "He who enlightens." (Vietnamese)

INTIFADA: "Shaking off," referring to the Arab uprising in the West Bank and Gaza Strip in December 1987 (Arabic)

MUJAHIDEEN: "Warriors of God" (Arabic)

SAMURAI: "One who serves" (Japanese)

SINN FEIN: "Ourselves Alone" (Gaelic)

STALIN: "Man of Steel" (Russian)

The Balfour Declaration

His Majesty's Government view with favour the establishment in Palestine of a national home for the Jewish people, and will use their best endeavours to facilitate the achievement of this object, it being clearly understood that nothing shall be done which may prejudice the civil and religious rights of existing non-Jewish communities in Palestine, or the rights and political status enjoyed by Jews in any other country.

—BRITISH FOREIGN SECRETARY ARTHUR JAMES BALFOUR,
NOVEMBER 2, 1917

Arab-Israeli Wars

1. Israel's War of Independence, 1948–49
2. Sinai War, 1956
3. Six-Day War, 1967

4. War of Attrition, 1969–70
5. Yom Kippur War, 1973
6. War in Lebanon, 1982

Nuclear Stockpiles, 2003

1. United States—7,206 warheads
2. Russian Federation—5,972 warheads
3. France—464 warheads
4. China—290 warheads
5. United Kingdom—185 warheads
6. Israel—150 warheads
7. India—60 warheads
8. Pakistan—24 warheads
9. North Korea—3 warheads

Medieval Arms and Equipment

ARBALEST: a hand crossbow
AVENTAIL: a medieval hood of mail suspended from a basinet to
    protect the neck and shoulders
BARDING: armor for horses
BASINET: an open-faced helmet
BASTARD SWORD: a long sword that could be wielded one- or
    two-handed
BRACER: a leather wrist guard used by archers
BUCKLER: a small, round shield
CALTROP: metal spikes that were placed on the ground to injure
    horses' hoofs
CAPARISON: padded cloth or leather covering for a warhorse
COIF: a chain mail hood
CUIRASS: plate armor for the chest and back
CULVERIN: the smallest variety of cannon

DESTRIER: a knight's warhorse

FALCHION: a curved short sword used by archers

FALCON: medium cannon

GLAIVE: a pole arm with curved blade

GREAVES: shin guards

HALBERD: a pole arm with an ax blade on one side of the head and a sharp spike on the other

HAUBERK: a chain mail shirt with long sleeves

HEATER: a shield with a straight top side and two curved sides meeting in a point at the bottom

JACK: quilted fabric used as armor by English archers

MISERICORD: a single-edged hiltless dagger used for giving the coup de grâce to the seriously injured

PENNON: a triangular flag carried on the end of a knight's lance

TARGET: a small, round shield

Scorched Earth Policies

1. SHERMAN'S MARCH TO THE SEA: After reducing much of Atlanta to ruins in 1864, General William Tecumseh Sherman began marching his 62,000 troops 250 miles to the coast across a 60-mile-wide front. He promised to "make Georgia howl" and burned or demolished virtually every bridge, railroad, factory, warehouse, and barn in his path.

2. CHINA: In July 1940 Japanese general Yasuji Okamura initiated a strategy he called "Take all, burn all, kill all" that reduced the Chinese population by several million in just eighteen months.

3. UKRAINE: In the face of the German advance in 1941, Soviet forces moved 6 million cattle, 550 large factories, thousands of small factories, 300,000 tractors, the country's entire railway rolling stock, and 3.5 million skilled workers to the Urals while destroying most of the infrastructure and resources that remained. During their own retreat in 1943–44, the Germans

razed 28,000 villages and 714 cities and towns, leaving 10 million people homeless.

4. KUWAIT: In their retreat from Kuwait in 1991, Iraqi forces sabotaged more than 700 of the country's oil wells, of which some 600 were set on fire.

5. AFGHANISTAN: In 1999, the Taliban looted and burned up to 300 houses a day in the north of the country to prevent fleeing refugees from returning.

6. EAST TIMOR: Before the Indonesian army ended its occupation of East Timor in 1999, it systematically burned most of the country's towns and villages, damaging or destroying 75 percent of Timorese buildings.

"The Feast of Crispian"

From *Henry V* by William Shakespeare, Act IV, scene III.

> King:
> This day is call'd the feast of Crispian:
> He that outlives this day, and comes safe home,
> Will stand a tip-toe when this day is nam'd,
> And rouse him at the name of Crispian.
> He that shall live this day, and see old age,
> Will yearly on the vigil feast his neighbours,
> And say, "To-morrow is Saint Crispian":
> Then will he strip his sleeve and show his scars,
> And say, "These wounds I had on Crispin's day."
> Old men forget: yet all shall be forgot,
> But he'll remember with advantages
> What feats he did that day. Then shall our names,
> Familiar in his mouth as household words,
> Harry the king, Bedford and Exeter,
> Warwick and Talbot, Salisbury and Gloucester,
> Be in their flowing cups freshly remember'd.

This story shall the good man teach his son;
And Crispin Crispian shall ne'er go by,
From this day to the ending of the world,
But we in it shall be remembered;
We few, we happy few, we band of brothers;
For he to-day that sheds his blood with me
Shall be my brother; be he ne'er so vile
This day shall gentle his condition:
And gentlemen in England now a-bed
Shall think themselves accurs'd they were not here,
And hold their manhoods cheap whiles any speaks
That fought with us upon Saint Crispin's day.

African Americans in the U.S. Army

War of Independence—5,000
Civil War—200,000
World War I—367,000
World War II—1,000,000
Korean War—3,100
Vietnam War—274,937
Persian Gulf War—104,000

U.S. Combat Deaths

WAR OF INDEPENDENCE (1775–83): 217,000 served; 4,435 killed
    in battle
WAR OF 1812 (1812–15): 286,730 served; 2,260 killed
INDIAN WARS (1817–90): approx. 106,000 served; approx. 1,000
    killed
MEXICAN WAR (1846–48): 78,789 served; 1,733 killed
CIVIL WAR (1861–65): 3,263,363 served; 214,938 killed
SPANISH-AMERICAN WAR (1898): 307,420 served; 385 killed

WORLD WAR I (1917–18): 4,743,826 served; 53,513 killed
WORLD WAR II (1941–45): 16,353,659 served; 292,131 killed
KOREAN WAR (1950–53): 5,764,143 served; 33,667 killed
VIETNAM WAR (1964–73): 8,752,000 served; 47,393 killed
PERSIAN GULF WAR (1991): 467,939 served; 148 killed

A U.S. Serviceman's Chances of Death in Battle

WAR OF INDEPENDENCE: 2 percent (a 1 in 50 chance)
WAR OF 1812: 0.8 percent (1 in 127)
INDIAN WARS: 0.9 percent (1 in 106)
MEXICAN WAR: 2.2 percent (1 in 45)
CIVIL WAR: 6.7 percent (1 in 15)
SPANISH-AMERICAN WAR: 0.1 percent (1 in 798)
WORLD WAR I: 1.1 percent (1 in 89)
WORLD WAR II: 1.8 percent (1 in 56)
KOREAN WAR: 0.6 percent (1 in 171)
VIETNAM WAR: 0.5 percent (1 in 185)
PERSIAN GULF WAR: 0.03 percent (1 in 3,162)

Other chances of death for an average American over his or her lifetime:

ACCIDENT (LAND, SEA, AIR): 1.3 percent (1 in 77)
SUICIDE: 0.8 percent (1 in 122)
MURDER: 0.5 percent (1 in 211)
NARCOTICS: 0.2 percent (1 in 592)
FISHING: 0.14 percent (1 in 714)

Living Veterans

Per 1990 census data; includes only veterans living in the United States and Puerto Rico. Extracted from Department of Veterans' Affairs.

Estimated number of living World War I veterans will be:

9/30/01	2,212	9/30/07	171	9/30/13	12
9/30/02	1,452	9/30/08	110	9/30/14	7
9/30/03	952	9/30/09	71	9/30/15	4
9/30/04	623	9/30/10	46	9/30/16	3
9/30/05	407	9/30/11	29	9/30/17	2
9/30/06	265	9/30/12	19	9/30/18	1

Estimated number of living World War II veterans will be:

9/30/01	5,032,591	9/30/08	2,383,578	9/30/15	724,947
9/30/02	4,618,560	9/30/09	2,074,699	9/30/16	583,410
9/30/03	4,211,991	9/30/10	1,788,795	9/30/17	463,088
9/30/04	3,815,644	9/30/11	1,526,903	9/30/18	362,282
9/30/05	3,432,216	9/30/12	1,289,627	9/30/19	279,113
9/30/06	3,064,236	9/30/13	1,077,141	9/30/20	211,584
9/30/07	2,714,009	9/30/14	889,152		

Some Notable War Films

All Quiet on the Western Front, dir. Lewis Milestone, 1930
Grand Illusion, dir. Jean Renoir, 1937
In Which We Serve, dir. Noël Coward and David Lean, 1942
The Cruel Sea, dir. Charles Frend, 1953

Stalag 17, dir. Billy Wilder, 1953
The Bridge on the River Kwai, dir. David Lean, 1957
Paths of Glory, dir. Stanley Kubrick, 1957
The Guns of Navarone, dir. J. Lee Thompson, 1961
Lawrence of Arabia, dir. David Lean, 1962
The Longest Day, dir. K. Annakin, A. Marton, B. Wicki, 1962
The Great Escape, dir. John Sturges, 1963
Zulu, dir. Cy Endfield, 1964
Dr. Strangelove, dir. Stanley Kubrick, 1964
Patton, dir. Franklin J. Schaffner, 1970
M*A*S*H, dir. Robert Altman, 1970
Cross of Iron, dir. Sam Peckinpah, 1977
The Deer Hunter, dir. Michael Cimino, 1978
Apocalypse Now, dir. Francis Ford Coppola, 1979
Das Boot, dir. Wolfgang Petersen, 1981
Full Metal Jacket, dir. Stanley Kubrick, 1987
Saving Private Ryan, dir. Steven Spielberg, 1998
Three Kings, dir. David O. Russell, 1999

Some Notable War Novels

War and Peace, by Leo Tolstoy, 1894
The Red Badge of Courage, by Stephen Crane, 1895
All Quiet on the Western Front, by Erich Maria Remarque, 1929
A Farewell to Arms, by Ernest Hemingway, 1929
For Whom the Bell Tolls, by Ernest Hemingway, 1940
The Naked and the Dead, by Norman Mailer, 1948
From Here to Eternity, by James Jones, 1951
Wheels of Terror, by Sven Hassel, 1959
Catch-22, by Joseph Heller, 1961
Slaughterhouse-Five, by Kurt Vonnegut, 1969
Regeneration, by Pat Barker, 1991
Birdsong, by Sebastian Faulks, 1993

What If?

Novels speculating on alternate military histories.

The Man in the High Castle, by Philip K. Dick: Germany takes the eastern United States, Japan the west

Fatherland, by Robert Harris: The Nazis win the war and occupy Britain

SS-GB, by Len Deighton: The Nazis win the war and occupy Britain

Guns of the South, by Harry Turtledove: Robert E. Lee wins the Civil War for the Confederacy

Ruled Britannia, by Harry Turtledove: The Spanish Armada conquers sixteenth-century England

Aztec Century, by Christopher Evans: The Aztecs invade Europe in the late twentieth century

Great Sieges

1. AZOTUS (NOW ASHDOD) IN ISRAEL, 664–610 B.C.: Besieged by Egyptian forces under Psamtik I for twenty-nine years.

2. SIEGE OF ATHENS, 404 B.C.: Brought the Athenian empire to an end, with the demolition of the city walls and the Spartan Lysander's imposition of the Thirty Tyrants' oligarchy.

3. CARTHAGE, 149–146 B.C.: The end of the siege marked the death of the Carthaginian civilization. The inhabitants of the capital were either killed or enslaved and its buildings razed to the ground.

4. MASADA, 73–74: The Judaean fortress of Masada was the last to be taken by the Romans as they reasserted imperial rule after the Jewish Rebellion. The 960 defenders committed mass suicide rather than surrender.

5. CANDIA (NOW HERAKLION, CRETE), 1648–69: The Turks besieged the Venetians for twenty-one years before their victory in 1669.

6. CONSTANTINOPLE (NOW ISTANBUL), 1453: Mehmed II of the

Turks used various tactics, including concentrated cannon fire to breach the walls and transporting his navy ten miles overland to attack the harbor, before a carelessly unlocked gate allowed the invaders into the city.

7. FORT SUMTER, 1863–65: Confederate forces endured one of the longest sieges in modern warfare during their occupancy of the stronghold. For 587 days from August 1863, 46,000 shells, estimated at more than 7 million pounds of metal, were fired at the defenders. The three-story structure was eventually reduced to rubble.

8. LENINGRAD, 1941–44: During an 880-day siege by the German army from August 30, 1941, until January 27, 1944, an estimated 1.4 million defenders and citizens died; 641,000 starved to death, while 17,000 died in artillery strikes. More than 150,000 shells and 100,000 bombs fell on the city.

9. STALINGRAD, 1943: The total death toll for the siege was 2,100,000. At the lifting of the siege, the civilian population stood at 1,515 from a prewar count of approximately 500,000.

10. SARAJEVO, MAY 2, 1992, TO FEBRUARY 26, 1996: The Yugoslav National Army besieged the capital of Bosnia-Herzegovina for a total of 1,395 days.

"The Battle of Britain Is about to Begin"

Excerpt from a speech given by Sir Winston Churchill to the House of Commons on June 18, 1940.

What General Weygand called the Battle of France is over. I expect that the Battle of Britain is about to begin. Upon this battle depends the survival of Christian civilization. Upon it depends our own British life, and the long continuity of our nation is turned on us. Hitler knows that he will have to break us in this Island or lose the war. If we can stand up to him, all Europe may be free and the life of the world may move forward into broad, sunlit uplands. But if we fail, then the whole world, including the United States, including all that we have known and cared for, will sink into the abyss of a new Dark Age made more sinister, and perhaps more protracted, by the light of perverted science. Let us therefore brace ourselves to our duties, and so bear ourselves that, if the British Empire and Commonwealth last for a thousand years, men will still say, This was their finest hour.

Six Confederate Units in the American Civil War

Tallapoosa Thrashers
Bartow Yankee Killers
Chickasaw Desperadoes
Lexington Wildcats
Raccoon Roughs
South Florida Bulldogs

Military Artisans, Engineers, and Designers

1. ARCHIMEDES: When the Romans under Marcus Claudius Marcellus laid siege to Syracuse in 213 B.C., the city's most famous inhabitant designed a range of stone- and dart-throwing machines that took a heavy toll on the attackers. Particularly feared was the Claw—a device lowered from the coastal walls that could capsize galleys.
2. CALLINICUS: The seventh-century Syrian engineer who invented Greek fire, the secret weapon of the eastern Roman emperors. The "liquid fire" was thrown by siphons onto ships, where it burst into flames on contact and was virtually inextinguishable, even on water.
3. MASTER URBAN: The Hungarian cannon maker could not find employment in the Byzantine empire, so he sold his services to the Turks, who used his giant weapons to breach the walls of Constantinople in 1452. Urban was killed during the siege when one of his creations exploded.

4. samuel colt: Patented the Colt revolver in 1836, the handgun that "made men equal."

5. dr. richard jordan gatling: Invented the world's first machine gun in 1862, a hand-cranked weapon at first rejected by the American Civil War forces of the time. Gatling initially trained as a medical doctor and came to firearms through designing farm machinery.

6. hiram maxim: The inventor of the Maxim gun was at the Paris Electrical Exhibition in 1881 when he was told: "If you want to make a lot of money, invent something that will enable these Europeans to cut each other's throats with greater facility."

7. anthony fokker: The Dutchman credited with devising a mechanical method of synchronizing machine-gun fire through the arc of an aircraft's propeller in 1914—a system used to great effect by the Germans on Fokker's monoplanes.

8. sir robert watson-watt: Credited with the production of a reliable RADAR system in 1935.

9. R. J. mitchell: Designer of the Spitfire fighter plane who died of cancer in 1937 before he could see the use to which it was put. Mitchell described the machine's title as "a bloody silly sort of name," and the Spitfire was almost named the Shrew.

10. barnes wallace: Designed the bouncing bombs used by 617 Squadron in the Dambusters raid to crack the Ruhr dams in 1943.

11. wernher von braun: Leader of the German team of scientists that designed the V2 ballistic missile in 1942 and who later helped build the Saturn V rocket that took America to the moon.

12. j. robert oppenheimer: American director of the Manhattan Project and builder of the first atomic bomb.

13. mikhail kalashnikov: Russian designer of the ubiquitous AK-47 assault rifle, of which more than 70 million have been produced worldwide since 1949.

14. j. mike o'dwyer: Australian inventor of "Metal Storm," the next-generation machine gun with no moving parts, which fires up to a million rounds a minute electronically.

Found in a Pillbox at Passchendaele in 1917 after Its Recapture by Allied Troops

Special orders to no.1 section.

1. This position will be held and the section will remain here until relieved.
2. The enemy cannot be allowed to interfere with this programme.
3. If this section cannot remain here alive it will remain here dead but in any case it will remain here.
4. Should any man through shell-shock or such cause attempt to surrender he will stay here dead.
5. Should all guns be blown out the section will use Mills grenades and other novelties.
6. Finally the position as stated will be held.

CAMPBELL CPL

Battle Tanks Compared

Machine Country Entered Service	Weight	Armor	Main Gun	Speed
FIRST WORLD WAR				
Mk 1 Britain 1916	62,720lb	12mm	2 × 6 pounder guns 4 × 8mm machine guns or 4 × 7.7mm machine guns, one 8mm machine gun	
Renault FT-17 France 1918	15,432lb	22mm	8mm machine gun	4.7mph
A7V Germany 1918	65,918lb	30mm	57mm	5mph

Machine Country Entered Service	Weight	Armor	Main Gun	Speed
SECOND WORLD WAR				
Char B1 France 1936	70,548lb	60mm	75mm	17mph
PzKpfw IV (Panzer Mk IV) Germany 1936	43,431lb	80mm	75mm	25mph
Type 97 Chi-Ha Japan 1938	33,069lb	25mm	57mm	24mph
A12 Matilda II Great Britain 1939	59,360lb	78mm	2 pounder	15mph
T-34/85 Soviet Union 1940	70,547lb	60mm	85mm	31mph
Carro Armato M13/40 Italy 1940	30,865lb	42mm	47mm	20mph
M4 Sherman United States 1942	69,565lb	76mm	75mm	26mph
PzKpfw VI Tiger I Germany 1942	121,253lb	100mm	88mm	24mph
IS-2 (Joseph Stalin) Soviet Union 1943	101,963lb	132mm	122mm	23mph
PzKpfw V Panther Germany 1943	98,766lb	100mm	75mm	29mph

Machine Country Entered Service	Weight	Armor	Main Gun	Speed
COLD WAR AND AFTER				
M60 United States 1960	108,000lb	120mm	105mm	30mph
T-62 Soviet Union 1963	80,468lb	170mm	115mm	31mph
Leopard I West Germany 1965	88,185lb	70mm	105mm	40mph
AMX-30 France 1967	79,366lb	50mm	105mm	40mph
Challenger II Great Britain 1991	137,789lb	(300mm)*	120mm	36mph
M1 A2 Abrams United States 1998	151,872lb	(300mm)*	120mm	42mph

*equivalent to 300mm conventional armor in terms of strength and effectiveness.

The Five Confederate Tribes

The Native American tribes given rights by the government of the Confederate States of America, which were denied them by the U.S. government. They served in cavalry units and as scouts. The Union victory deprived the tribes of their remaining rights, leaving them worse off than before their involvement in the American Civil War.

Cherokee	Choctaw	Seminole
Chickasaw	Creek	

Second World War Conferences

1. MOSCOW, SEPTEMBER 29–OCTOBER 1, 1941: Conferees: Stalin, Harriman, Beaverbrook. Allied aid to Russia organized.

2. WASHINGTON (ARCADIA), DECEMBER 22, 1941–JANUARY 14, 1942: Churchill, Roosevelt. The United States agrees to follow Churchill's "Europe first" strategy; Declaration of the United Nations.

3. WASHINGTON (2ND), JUNE 20–25, 1942: Churchill, Roosevelt. Agreed to share the research needed for the development of the A-bomb "as equal partners." North Africa given temporary priority over a cross-channel invasion.

4. CASABLANCA (SYMBOL), JANUARY 14–24, 1943: Churchill, Roosevelt. Plans made for invasion of Sicily and Italy; invasion of France scheduled for 1944; Allies demand "unconditional surrender" from the Axis powers.

5. BERMUDA, APRIL 1943: Held by the United States and Great Britain to discuss the ways to help European Jews in the shadow of the Holocaust. Its only achievement was to open a refugee center in North Africa.

6. WASHINGTON (TRIDENT), MAY 12–27, 1943: Churchill, Roosevelt. Main result: Invasion of Italy planned; increased aggression in the Pacific theater; increased air attacks on Germany

7. QUEBEC (QUADRANT), AUGUST 17–24, 1943: Churchill, Roosevelt. Main results: D-day planned; Southeast Asia command reorganized for war on Japan; Gilbert Islands and Marshall Islands set as first objectives in Pacific offensive.

8. MOSCOW, OCTOBER 18–NOVEMBER 1, 1943: Allied foreign secretaries Hull, Eden, Molotov. Postwar cooperation in Europe broached.

9. CAIRO (SEXTANT), NOVEMBER 23–26, 1943: Churchill, Roosevelt, Chiang Kai-shek. Military operations in China planned against the Japanese; postwar return of Manchuria to China and freedom for Korea promised.

10. TEHRAN (EUREKA), NOVEMBER 28–DECEMBER 1, 1943: Churchill, Roosevelt, Stalin. Two-front war against Germany planned, along with later Russian participation in war against Japan.

11. CAIRO (2ND) DECEMBER 4–6, 1943: Churchill, Roosevelt, Ismet Inonu: Eisenhower given supreme Allied command.

12. Quebec (OCTAGON), September 12–16, 1944: Churchill, Roosevelt, King. Attack on Greece and Istria and occupation of postwar Germany planned.

13. YALTA (ARGONAUT), FEBRUARY 4–11, 1945: Churchill, Roosevelt, Stalin. Postwar policy agreed upon, including formation of the United Nations and conditions under which Russia would enter the war against Japan.

14. POTSDAM (TERMINAL), JULY 17–AUGUST 2, 1945: Truman, Stalin, Churchill (Attlee after British election). Japanese surrender demanded; agreement on principles governing treatment of Germany.

Poets Corner

Poets and writers of World War I commemorated in Poet's Corner, Westminster Abbey, London.

Richard Aldington	David Jones
Laurence Binyon	Robert Nichols
Edmund Blunden	Wilfred Owen*
Rupert Brooke*	Herbert Read
Wilfrid Gibson	Isaac Rosenberg*
Robert Graves	Siegfried Sassoon
Julian Grenfell*	Charles Sorley*
Ivor Gurney	Edward Thomas*

*Died during the war.

Notable War Correspondents and Photographers

1. WILLIAM HOWARD RUSSELL: The London *Times*'s man in Crimea covered the charge of the Light Brigade and exposed both the suffering of the ordinary soldiers and the incompetence of their leaders.

2. ARCHIBALD FORBES: Witnessed Napoleon III's surrender to Bismarck in a weaver's cottage during the Franco-Prussian War and in 1879 once rode through ten miles of Zulu territory to a telegraph office where he could report on the Battle of Ulundi.

3. JANUARIUS ALOYSIUS MACGAHAN: The crusading Irish-American newsman revealed the 1876 massacre of 12,000 Bulgarian men, women, and children at the hands of Kurdish forces commanded by Turkey.

4. STEPHEN CRANE: The author of *The Red Badge of Courage* covered the charge up San Juan hill by the Rough Riders and personally received the surrender of the town of Juana Diaz during the Spanish-American War of 1898.

5. CORA CRANE: Stephen Crane's wife, Cora, formerly the madam of an elegant brothel, was billed as the first female war correspondent. Writing for the New York press under the pen name Imogene Carter, she went with her husband to cover the Greco-Turkish war. After he died, she attempted a literary career of her own, unsuccessfully, then opened her second brothel in Jacksonville, Florida.

6. LUIGI BARZINI: The Italian reporter wrote of the brutality with which European troops put down the Boxer Rising in China and told of the birth of the modern battlefield during the Russo-Japanese War of 1904.

7. WINSTON CHURCHILL: Reported from, as well as participated in, the Battle of Omdurman and the Boer War.

8. ROBERT CAPA: The photographer most famous for his coverage of the Spanish Civil War and the D-day landings.

9. MARTHA GELLHORN: The veteran reporter who covered conflicts from the Spanish Civil War to the U.S. invasion of Panama when she was eighty-one.

10. ALAN MOOREHEAD: Chronicled the North African campaign of World War II in his classic *African Trilogy*.

11. DITH PRAN: A Cambodian who remained in Phnom Penh to report on the fall of the city in 1975 and was subsequently interned in a Khmer Rouge reeducation camp. He later escaped to the United States.

12. MICHAEL HERR: An American journalist who wrote of drug-addled grunts in jungle combat in *Dispatches,* his account of the Vietnam War.

13. DON MCCULLIN: British photographer most famous for his unflinching coverage of the Vietnam War.

14. JON PILGER: An Australian broadcaster and war correspondent who has reported from many countries including Vietnam and Cambodia.

Notable Bridges and Bridgeheads

1. XERXES' PONTOON: In 480 B.C., Xerxes of Persia and his armies crossed the Hellespont, the strait separating Europe from Asia, on a floating bridge of 674 boats, tied together to make two parallel bridges, each with a length of nearly a mile.

2. CAESAR AND THE RHINE: In 55 B.C. Julius Caesar constructed a bridge across the upper Rhine in ten days. The German tribes on the far bank were so in awe of this feat of engineering that they submitted to Roman power. Caesar dismantled the bridge and returned home having won without fighting a battle.

3. THE POTOMAC PONTOON: In 1864, Union army engineers constructed a 2,170-foot pontoon bridge of 68 boats linked by planks across the James River to enable Grant's Army of the Potomac,

comprising some 45,000 men and 30,000 horses, to attack Petersburg, Virginia, and cut off the Confederate army's supply line.

4. THE BRIDGE ON THE RIVER KWAI: 260 miles long and built in sixteen months beginning in October 1942. The total labor force consisted of about 68,000 Allied POWs and 200,000 Asian laborers, of whom 18,000 and 78,000, died respectively.

5. A BRIDGE TOO FAR: In September 1944, British and Polish paratroopers were charged with taking the bridge at Arnhem and holding it for forty-eight hours until armored support arrived. Lieutenant Colonel John Frost's battalion was the only one that reached the bridge, which it defended for seven days though the promised support never arrived.

6. REMAGEN BRIDGE: In the spring of 1945 the U.S. Ninth Armored Division took the Ludendorff railway bridge at Remagen, Germany in a surprise attack. Brigadier General Hoge proceeded against orders and raced units across before the Germans could detonate charges placed on the bridge.

7. THE SAVA RIVER CROSSING: Twenty thousand vehicles including the U.S. Army's First Armored Division crossed the Sava River between Croatia and Bosnia and Herzegovina on a pontoon bridge 650 yards long amid severe floods in 1995.

Amazon Women

Amazon = "no breast" in Ancient Greek.

1. CAUCASIANS: A tribe of warrior women who lived between the Black and Caspian seas along the Thermidon River in around 8000 B.C. At the age of eight, each girl had her right breast seared with a hot iron so that no mammary glands would grow to impede the use of a bow. The procedure was also believed to extirpate the masculine tendencies that were thought to emanate from the right side.

2. LIBYANS: A pre-Homeric tribe that lived along the Atlas Mountains of Morocco and wore red leather armor in battle.

3. GAGANS: North African Amazons who, until the tribe converted to Christianity, routinely killed baby boys.

4. HAMITICS: A tribe that lived between the Nile and the Red Sea.

5. SAUROMATIANS: A tribe that lived along the Don River in Russia. According to Herodotus, these women were not permitted to bear children until they had killed three male enemies.

6. EURYPLE'S AMAZONS: The tribe that captured Babylon in 1760 B.C.

7. THE AMAZON'S AMAZONS: A tribe that attacked Portuguese explorers in the 1500s along the Amazon River.

Battlefield Trophies

1. ARMOR: From the ancient world to the Middle Ages, one of the chief tasks of a fighting man's squire was to strip his defeated opponents of their valuable armor as they lay on the battlefield.

2. ROMAN EAGLES: Two eagle standards were taken by the barbarian forces of Arminius after the defeat of Varus in A.D. 9. They were recovered by Germanicus in A.D. 15 or 16.

3. EARS: After the Battle of Leigniz in 1241 the Mongols collected nine sacks of severed ears from the defeated forces of the Teutonic Knights.

4. SPURS: In 1302 an army sent by Philip IV of France to put down the rebellious Flemish towns led by Bruges was comprehensively defeated. The spurs taken from the fallen French knights formed so large a mound that the battle was named after them.

5. SCALPS: Taken by Native American tribes and also by the ancient Scythians, who made them into napkins and decorative clothing.

6. SHRUNKEN HEADS: The Jivaro tribesmen of Ecuador traditionally decapitated their enemies and shrank the heads to the size of an orange; these were then worn like medals.

7. LUGERS: The German army issue automatic pistol was the most prized trophy for Allied troops during World War II. However, many who acquired one were injured due to the difficulty of operating its safety mechanism.

8. BONES: Skulls, vertebrae, and other bones from dead Japanese servicemen were taken as souvenirs by U.S. troops in the Pacific theater during World War II. One lieutenant's young girlfriend posed with a skull she dubbed "Tojo" for *Life* magazine's "photo of the week."

9. TEETH: A valuable commodity in the 1700s, healthy teeth extracted from dead soldiers were fashioned into "Waterloo dentures."

10. GENITALIA: Around 1300 B.C., King Menephta's army returned to Egypt with 13,000 severed phalluses taken from the defeated Libyans. Details were inscribed on a monument at Karnak: Libyan generals 6; Libyans 6,539; Sirculians 222; Etruscans 542; Greeks 6,111.

11. "SNIPERS' HELMETS": After the World War I armistice was signed, the young Walt Disney made money by taking new army helmets and adding bullet holes, blood, hair, and earth and selling them as battlefield remains.

The Decalogue: The Ten Commandments of the Knightly Code of Chivalry

1. Thou shalt believe all that the Church teaches, and shalt observe all its directions.
2. Thou shalt defend the Church.
3. Thou shalt respect all weaknesses, and shalt constitute thyself the defender of them.
4. Thou shalt love the country in which thou wast born.
5. Thou shalt not recoil before thine enemy.
6. Thou shalt make war against the Infidel without cessation, and without mercy.

7. Thou shalt perform scrupulously thy feudal duties, if they be not contrary to the laws of God.

8. Thou shalt never lie, and shall remain faithful to thy pledged word.

9. Thou shalt be generous, and give largesse to everyone.

10. Thou shalt be everywhere and always the champion of the Right and the Good against Injustice and Evil.

Young Lions

Precocious military commanders.

1. STEPHEN OF CLOYES: In 1212 the twelve-year-old French shepherd led an army of several thousand boys to retake the holy land in the Children's Crusade. Stephen expected the waters of the Mediterranean to part for his advance, but when they did not, merchants offered to transport his forces across the sea free of charge. Once the children reached Brindisi, many were sold as slaves to the Moors, while the rest starved to death.

2. GENERAL MARQUIS DE GILBERT DU MOTIER LAFAYETTE: The twenty-year-old French "Boy General" commanded a reconnaissance force for George Washington during the American Revolutionary War and once led a successful breakout when his 2,000 troops were encircled by an army eight times their size.

3. GALUSHA PENNYPACKER: In 1863 the twenty-three-year-old George Armstrong Custer was the youngest general in the Union army. However, in 1865 Galusha Pennypacker was promoted to brigadier general one month before his twenty-first birthday—a U.S. Army record that has stood ever since.

4. JOEL IGLESIAS: The young Cuban communist was only fifteen years old when he joined Fidel Castro's rebels in 1957 and was

an army commander when the revolutionary forces entered Havana in 1959.

5. CAPTAIN VALENTINE STRASSER: In 1992 Sierra Leone's president Joseph Momoh fled the statehouse when a delegation of army officers led by Strasser arrived to protest over late wages. The twenty-six-year-old captain and champion disco dancer seized the chance to make himself military dictator of the country, which he went on to rule for four years.

6. JOHNNY AND LUTHER HTOO: Twin boys who led the ethnic Keren "God's Army" rebel force against Myanmar's military junta. They claimed to be fourteen years old when they surrendered in 2001 but they were only eight, according to other sources. Their Christian fundamentalist troops believed the boys to be divinely inspired.

The Ten Costliest Battles of the U.S. Civil War

1. Gettysburg, July 1–3, 1863
   51,112 casualties (23,049 Union and 28,063 Confederate)
2. Chickamauga, September 19–20, 1863
   34,624 (16,170 Union and 18,454 Confederate)
3. Chancellorsville, May 1–4, 1863
   30,099 (17,278 Union and 12,821 Confederate)
4. Spotsylvania, May 8–19, 1864
   27,399 (18,399 Union and 9,000 Confederate)
5. Antietam, September 17, 1862
   26,134 (12,410 Union and 13,724 Confederate)
6. The Wilderness, May 5–7, 1864
   25,416 (17,666 Union and 7,750 Confederate)
7. Second Manassas, or Bull Run, August 29–30, 1862
   25,251 (16,054 Union and 9,197 Confederate)
8. Murfreesboro, or Stones River, December 31, 1862 and January 2, 1863
   24,645 (12,906 Union and 11,739 Confederate)

9. Shiloh, April 6–7, 1862
   23,741 (13,047 Union and 10,694 Confederate)
10. Fort Donelson, February 12–16, 1862
    19,455 (2,832 Union and 16,623 Confederate)

Fighting on the Beaches

From a speech by Winston Churchill on June 4, 1940.

> We shall not flag or fail. We shall go on to the end. We shall fight in France. We shall fight on the seas and oceans. We shall fight with growing confidence and growing strength in the air. We shall defend our island, whatever the cost may be. We shall fight on the beaches. We shall fight on the landing grounds. We shall fight in the fields and in the streets. We shall fight in the hills. We shall never surrender, and even if, which I do not for a moment believe, this Island or a large part of it were subjugated and starving, then our Empire beyond the seas, armed and guarded by the British fleet, would carry on the struggle, until, in God's good time, the New World, with all its power and might, steps forth to the rescue and the liberation of the old.

Cannon Ammunition in the Age of Sail

1. ROUND SHOT: Stone balls before the seventeenth century, iron afterward. These were used against the wooden hulls of enemy ships.
2. CHAIN SHOT: Two small round shot linked by a length of chain. This was used to slash through the rigging and sails of opposing ships.
3. CANISTER SHOT: Several hundred musket balls packed into a tin canister. Used mainly on land.

4. SPHERICAL CASE SHOT, OR SHRAPNEL: A hollow round shell packed with musket balls and a bursting charge, which exploded over the heads of the enemy.
5. GRAPE SHOT: Mainly used at sea, and consisting of a canvas bag filled with nine golf ball–sized solid balls, usually aimed at rigging and spars.

America's Wars and Foreign Interventions

1. The American Revolution, 1775–83 v. Great Britain
2. Indian Wars, 1775–1890 v. Native Americans
3. Quasi-War, 1798–1800 v. France
4. Barbary Wars, 1800–1815 v. the Barbary States (Tripoli, Algiers, and Morocco)
5. War of 1812, 1812–15 v. Great Britain
6. Mexican-American War, 1846–48 v. Mexico
7. Intervention in Hawaiian Revolution, 1893 v. Hawaiian government
8. Spanish-American War, 1898 v. Spain
9. Intervention in Samoan Civil War, 1898–99 v. German-backed forces
10. U.S.-Philippine War, 1899–1902 v. Philippines
11. Boxer Rebellion, 1900 v. China
12. Moro Wars, 1901–13 v. Moslem Filipinos
13. Intervention in Panamanian Revolution, 1903 v. Colombia
14. The Banana Wars, 1909–33 v. Central American rebels
15. Occupation of Vera Cruz, 1914 v. Mexico
16. Pershing's raid into Mexico, 1916–17 v. Mexico
17. World War I, 1917–18 v. Germany
18. Intervention in Russian Civil War, 1919–21 v. Bolsheviks
19. World War II, 1941–45 v. Germany, Japan, Italy
20. Korean War, 1950–53 v. North Korea and China
21. Intervention in Lebanon, 1958 v. antigovernment rebels

22. Vietnam War, 1964–73 v. North Vietnam and South Vietnamese rebels
23. Intervention in the Dominican Republic, 1965 v. antigovernment rebels
24. Bombing of Libya, 1981 and 1986 v. Colonel Gadhafi's regime
25. Intervention in Lebanon, 1982–84 v. Syria, and terrorist groups
26. Invasion of Grenada, 1983 v. Cubans and Grenadine communists
27. The Tanker War, 1987–88 v. Iran
28. Invasion of Panama, 1989 v. General Manuel Noriega's regime
29. Persian Gulf War, 1991 v. Iraq
30. Intervention in Somalia, 1992–94 v. Somali militia groups
31. Intervention in Bosnia, 1994–95 v. Bosnian Serbs
32. Occupation of Haiti, 1994 v. Haitian regime
33. Bombing of Afghanistan and Sudan, 1998 v. terrorist groups
34. Operation Desert Fox, 1998 v. Iraq
35. Kosovo War, 1999 v. Serbia
36. Afghanistan War, 2001 v. Taliban and Al Qa'ida
37. Iraq War, 2003 v. Iraq

America's Civil Wars and Rebellions

1. SHAYS'S REBELLION, 1786–87: rebels v. the state government of Massachusetts.
2. THE WHISKEY REBELLION, 1794: tax revolt in western Pennsylvania.
3. FRIES'S REBELLION ("THE HOT WATER WAR"), 1799: tax revolt in Pennsylvania.
4. SLAVE REBELLIONS, 1800–65: African-American slaves.
5. "BLEEDING KANSAS," 1855–60: proslavery v. antislavery Kansans.
6. BROWN'S RAID ON HARPERS FERRY, 1859: rebellion against slavery led by John Brown.
7. UNITED STATES CIVIL WAR, 1861–65: Union (northern) states v. Confederate (southern) states.

Largest Battleships

Vessel class	Nation	Year	Weight (tons)	Dimensions (feet)	Crew	Main guns	Speed (knots)
Yamato	Japan	1940	62,315	868×121	2,500	9×18.1in	27*
Iowa	United States	1943	48,110	887×108	1,921	9×16in	33
Vanguard	Great Britain	1944	44,500	814×108	1,893	8×15in	30
Hood	Great Britain	1918	42,450	860×104	1,480	8×15in	32
Bismarck	Germany	1939	41,700	824×118	2,100	8×15in	30
Vittorio Veneto	Italy	1937	40,517	779×108	1,850	9×15in	30
South Dakota	United States	1941	37,970	680×108	1,793	9×16in	28
King George V	Great Britain	1939	36,727	745×103	1,422	10×14in	29
Richelieu	France	1939	35,000	813×108	1,670	8×15in	30
Scharnhorst	Germany	1936	34,850	754×98	1,670	9×11in	32

*During the Battle of Leyte Gulf in October 1944, it took 19 torpedoes and 17 bombs to sink the *Musashi*.

Marching Rates

Paces per minute.

Napoleonic Grande Armée—120
U.S. Army—120
Chinese People's Liberation Army—108
Ancient Roman Legion—100
French Foreign Legion—88
British Army under Wellington—75

Accidents at Sea

Ships sunk or damaged without enemy action.

1. The *Mary Rose:* In 1545, Henry VIII's overloaded flagship wheeled in the wind and sank as water rushed into the lower gun ports that the crew had omitted to close.
2. The *Wasa:* The 64-gun Swedish flagship sank on her maiden voyage in 1628, capsizing in the wind almost as soon as her sails were hoisted.
3. The *Kronan:* The Swedish admiral Baron Lorentz Creutz's last words were, "In the name of Jesus, make sure that the cannon ports are closed and the cannon made fast, so that in turning we don't suffer the same fate as befell the *Wasa*." The ports were not closed and his flagship sank in 1675 as had her predecessor about fifty years earlier.
4. HMS *Association:* In 1707 the British Mediterranean commander Sir Cloudesley Shovell was returning home late in the season when his squadron misjudged their longitude and were wrecked on the Isles of Scilly. This disaster led the government to offer sponsorship for research into a reliable method of determining longitude, resulting in John Harrison's chronometer.

5. HMS *Victoria:* In an exercise in the Bay of Tripoli in 1893, Admiral Sir George Tryon of the Royal Navy put his flagship on a collision course with HMS *Camperdown.* He refused to reverse his orders despite the warnings of his officers and was reported to have said "It is all my fault" before he drowned with 358 other seamen.

6. *U-28:* During World War I, the German submarine launched a close-range surface attack on the British cargo ship *Olive Branch.* When a shell from the *U-28*'s deck gun set off a consignment of ammunition aboard the ship, the explosion was enough to sink the attacking submarine.

7. HMS *Trinidad:* In 1941 the Royal Navy submarine fired a torpedo at a German destroyer only for the weapon to describe a curving course, returning to destroy the *Trinidad*'s engine room and put her out of the war. The same fate was suffered by the American submarine USS *Tang,* which torpedoed itself in the Formosa Strait in 1944.

8. K-141 *Kursk:* The nuclear-powered Russian submarine sank with all hands in the Barents Sea in 2000 after an explosion in one of her torpedo tubes. Russian authorities have claimed this was due to a collision with a foreign vessel—an account dismissed by international investigators.

Quotations

Dulce et decorum est pro patria mori (It is a sweet and seemly thing to die for one's country).

—HORACE, *ODES*, III

I want you to remember that no son of a bitch ever won a war by dying for his country. He won it by making the other poor dumb bastard die for his country.

—GENERAL GEORGE S. PATTON

O people, know that you have committed great sins and that the great ones among you have committed these sins. If you ask me what proof I have for these words, I say it is because I am the punishment of God. If you had not committed great sins, God would not have sent a punishment like me upon you.

—GENGHIS KHAN TO THE SURVIVORS
OF HIS SACK OF BUKHARA, 1220

Veni, vidi, vici (I came, I saw, I conquered).

—JULIUS CAESAR AFTER DEFEATING KING PHARNACES II
IN ASIA MINOR, 47 B.C.

I would like to see the clause in Adam's will which excludes France from the division of the world.

—FRANCIS I (1494–1547)

Going to war without France is like going deer hunting without your accordion.

—H. NORMAN SCHWARZKOPF

I know I have the body of a weak and feeble woman, but I have the heart and stomach of a king, and of a king of England too; and think foul scorn that Parma or Spain, or any prince of Europe, should dare to invade the borders of my realm.

—QUEEN ELIZABETH I TO THE ARMY AT TILBURY AS THE
SPANISH ARMADA APPROACHED ENGLAND IN 1588

It takes a brave man not to be a hero in the Red Army.

—JOSEPH STALIN

Pour encourager les autres (to encourage the others).

—VOLTAIRE ON THE EXECUTION OF ADMIRAL BYNG
IN 1757 FOR HAVING RETREATED IN THE FACE
OF THE ENEMY

Oh! he is mad, is he? Then I wish he would bite some of my other generals.

—GEORGE II, REPLYING TO ADVISERS WHO TOLD
HIM THAT GENERAL JAMES WOLFE WAS INSANE

Qui desiderat pacem, praeparet bellum (Let him who desires peace prepare for war).

—VEGETIUS, FOURTH CENTURY

Political power grows out of the barrel of a gun.

—MAO TSE-TUNG

I hope to God I have fought my last battle . . . I am wretched even at the moment of victory, and I always say that next to a battle lost, the greatest misery is a battle gained.

—THE DUKE OF WELLINGTON AFTER WATERLOO

Ours is composed of the scum of the earth—the mere scum of the earth. The British soldiers are fellows who have all enlisted for drink—that is the plain fact—they have all enlisted for drink.

—WELLINGTON DESCRIBING THE BRITISH ARMY, 1811

It takes 15,000 casualties to train a major general.

—FERDINAND FOCH

An army marches on its stomach.

—NAPOLEON

C'est magnifique, mais ce n'est pas la guerre (It is magnificent, but it is not war).

—PIERRE BOSQUET AFTER WITNESSING THE CHARGE
OF THE LIGHT BRIGADE, OCTOBER 25, 1854

War is an ugly thing, but not the ugliest of things. The decayed and degraded state of moral and patriotic feeling, which thinks that nothing is worth war, is much worse. The person who has nothing for which he is willing to fight, nothing which is more important than his own personal safety, is a miserable creature and has no chance of being free unless made and kept so by the exertions of better men than himself.

—JOHN STUART MILL, 1868

Nuts!

—MAJOR GENERAL ANTHONY MCAULIFFE, U.S. ARMY, DECEMBER 23, 1944, IN RESPONSE TO THE DEMAND THAT HE SURRENDER HIS SURROUNDED TROOPS AT BASTOGNE

A great part of the information obtained in war is contradictory, a still greater part is false, and by far the greatest part is of a doubtful character.

—CARL VON CLAUSEWITZ, ON WAR, 1832

Don't talk to me about Naval tradition. It's nothing but rum, sodomy and the lash.

—WINSTON CHURCHILL TO THE BOARD OF ADMIRALTY, 1939

Young man, you did a very fine thing to give up a most promising career to fight for your country. Mark you, had you not done so, it would have been despicable.

—WINSTON CHURCHILL TO DAVID NIVEN

Peccavi (I have sinned).

—GENERAL NAPIER'S ALLEGED DISPATCH UPON CAPTURING THE INDIAN PROVINCE OF SINDH, 1843

I shall return.

—DOUGLAS MACARTHUR UPON LEAVING THE PHILIPPINES AHEAD OF THE JAPANESE INVASION FORCE, 1942 (HE DID RETURN, IN 1944)

I thought he was talking about our mess bill.

—ANONYMOUS RAF PILOT UPON HEARING CHURCHILL'S
SPEECH CONTAINING THE LINES "NEVER IN THE FIELD
OF HUMAN CONFLICT HAS SO MUCH BEEN OWED BY SO
MANY TO SO FEW"

You know, Mr. Frost, at Spandau we grew tomatoes und we
were not allowed to give these tomatoes to the old people of
Spandau because they had been grown by the war criminals. So
they were taken out und burnt. Mr. Frost, do you realize what it
can do to a man to have his tomatoes burnt?

—NAZI WAR CRIMINAL BALDUR VON SCHIRACH
TO INTERVIEWER DAVID FROST

Women would make a grand brigade, if it was not for snakes and
spiders. They don't mind bullets—women are not afraid of bullets;
but one big black-snake would put a whole army to flight.

—CSA LIEUTENANT GENERAL RICHARD EWELL

You have lost your left arm. I have lost my right arm.

—ROBERT E. LEE TO STONEWALL JACKSON AFTER
THE LATTER WAS MAIMED AT CHANCELLORSVILLE

We'll start the war from here!

—BRIGADIER GENERAL THEODORE ROOSEVELT JR. ON
LANDING ON UTAH BEACH, JUNE 6, 1944

In wartime truth is so precious that she should always be
attended by a bodyguard of lies.

—WINSTON CHURCHILL

By the time you get this, I may be a heap of rotting carrion on a
field in Mexico.

—GEORGE S. PATTON IN A LETTER HOME TO HIS FAMILY

Overpaid, oversexed and over here.
> —POPULAR BRITISH DESCRIPTION OF AMERICAN
> SERVICEMEN IN WORLD WAR II

Men go into the Navy thinking they will enjoy it. They do enjoy it for about a year, at least the stupid ones do, riding back and forth quite dully on ships. The bright ones find that they don't like it in half a year, but there's always the thought of that pension if only they stay in . . . Gradually they become crazy. Crazier and crazier. Only the Navy has no way of distinguishing between the sane and the insane. Only about 5 percent of the Royal Navy have the sea in their veins. They are the ones who become captains. Thereafter, they are segregated on their bridges. If they are not mad before this, they go mad then. And the maddest of these become admirals.
> —GEORGE BERNARD SHAW

He's either never been to Umm Qasar or he's never been to Southampton. There's no beer, no prostitutes and people are shooting at us. It's more like Portsmouth.
> —BRITISH TROOPER AFTER GEOFF HOON, THE DEFENSE
> MINISTER, HAD COMPARED THE IRAQI PORT TO
> THE ENGLISH COASTAL TOWN

They couldn't hit an elephant at this dist . . .
> —LAST WORDS OF UNION ARMY GENERAL JOHN SEDGWICK, 1864

SOURCES

The material in this book was compiled from several hundred sources. The most up-to-date figures and most comprehensive information have been given wherever possible. This has meant that data and statistics from different authorities have had to be combined in tables and lists that therefore cannot be attributed to a single origin for research purposes. However, among the most useful reference books were the *CIA World Fact Book,* 2002, the *SIPRI Yearbook,* 2002, *Cassell's History of Warfare* series, and the Jane's series of defense titles. The Imperial War Museum, London, has been an invaluable resource. Many conflicting versions of historical events and statistics exist, and in these cases the most widely agreed upon information has been favored.

ACKNOWLEDGMENTS

Special thanks go to Angus MacKinnon, Penny Gardiner, and Gordon Corrigan for their work in editing this book, to Philip Lewis for the jacket and text design, to Alpha Graphics for the typesetting, to Brando Skyhorse for help with the U.S. edition, and to Toby Mundy and Bonnie Chiang for overseeing the project from start to finish.